The Untold Stories of the Middle East

A new generation shaping the region

Written by Olivia Cuthbert

IDEAS beyond borders

Copyright © 2024 by Ideas Beyond Borders, Inc.

Published by House of Wisdom 2.0 Press, an imprint of Ideas Beyond Borders.

All rights reserved. No part of this book may be reproduced in any matter without the prior written permission of the publisher, except for brief quotations in articles, reviews and social media. For information, please address House of Wisdom 2.0 Press, Ideas Beyond Borders, 244 Fifth Avenue, Suite 2594, New York, NY 10001.

Creative direction and design by Mariana Bernardez.

Cover illustration and other Illustrations by Lana Al-Jaf.

All photography in this book noted where relevant. Particular thanks to:
Osama Al Maqdoni in Iraq, Natheer Halawani in Lebanon, and Paeez Jahanbin in Afghanistan.

Text by Olivia Cuthbert, editing by Reid Newton, sub-editing by Jacqueline Castelluccia

The Untold Stories of the Middle East
By Ideas Beyond Borders, Inc.

ISBN 9798329653366

House of Wisdom 2.0 Press
Ideas Beyond Borders
244 Fifth Avenue, Suite 2594
New York, NY 10001
ideasbeyondborders.org

For people with bold ideas building a better future
in the Middle East and Afghanistan

Table of Contents

Foreword	p. 01
Remodeling development	pp. 02-05
The Innovation Hub in action	pp. 06-09
Iraq	pp. 10-37
Kurdistan	pp. 38-59
Afghanistan	pp. 60-87
Lebanon	pp. 88-111
Crisis response	pp. 112-129
Author's note	pp. 130-131
People of the Innovation Hub	pp. 132-133

IDEAS BEYOND BORDERS

Foreword

Written into the DNA of Ideas Beyond Borders is that we are here, first and foremost, to solve problems. We don't just advocate for solutions; rather, we ourselves are the problem solvers. The ultimate goal of this organization is that there ceases to be a need for us anymore—we aim to give power to the people living in MENA so that they can flourish without external intervention.

Growing up in Iraq, I witnessed firsthand the red tape that surrounds obtaining funds for any project, large or small. Only the elite, who were familiar with the boilerplate development jargon organizations sought, and who were well connected to those in power, received funds to launch projects, reinforcing the political, religious and economic divisions that segregate society.

That's where IBB's Innovation Hub comes in. We are able to identify talent and endorse potential without requiring a 30-page proposal. We take risks on people and projects we believe in because our grants are given in small amounts, but arguably go further toward bettering communities than large sums that disappear into a vast project and yield few tangible results.

Fifteen years ago, I was one of these citizens with an idea. I wasn't part of the elite, nor was I well-connected. Nevertheless, today, I am the President and Co-founder of a thriving nonprofit organization that brings knowledge and resources to areas in the Middle East that need it the most. I am keenly aware of what is possible if you offer belief in an idea and potential for success. Those who know how to obtain funding and launch a project don't need us—the Innovation Hub targets those who need the support. Our job is to make it as easy as possible for them to succeed. Our credibility comes from our grantees doing what they said they would do with our support, and we are cautious about who we choose. We look for people who have ambition, energy, and the will to get things done.

The Innovation Hub was born in 2021 and has grown exponentially since then. One of the things I love most about the project is that it gives us a realistic pulse of what the region needs most. We are witnessing the great level of innovation and energy that people have despite ongoing wars and conflict. Connecting with these people and hearing their stories fills me with enthusiasm and hope for the future.

We're operating in a supply and demand situation, and those in the West often miscalculate what is required. Rather than impose what we think a specific region, country, or town needs, we listen to the people who face these challenges daily.

High levels of corruption are one of the reasons why unemployment is a significant issue in MENA. We choose to support small businesses for a specific reason: to avoid becoming a part of the problem ourselves. When development money is given to a country like Iraq, and Iraqis see no progress, anti-West sentiment grows. They see this money (often millions of dollars) going directly into the pockets of militia groups and corrupt political parties. When it comes to allocating Innovation Hub funds, our vetting process makes sure this doesn't happen.

We are moving more and more into the private sector, where demand is growing. People cannot begin thinking about enlightenment values if they can't first put food on the table. By supporting businesses like Kurd Wears, a clothing company that employs locals and sells its products abroad, we are creating sustainable change where each generation builds on the last. This is where the impact lies.

As governments like Kurdistan's move away from oil and turn toward the private sector, IBB stands ready to bridge the gap and help people start their businesses. What I love about the Middle East is that—despite the narratives pushed by extremists—people are resilient, anxiously awaiting their opportunity to be a part of the solution.

Building on a sturdy foundation takes time, but already we see signs of progress as the people we support become more self-sufficient. Refugees we work with are less dependent on aid. Working-class people are less dependent on government jobs, and people employed by the businesses we fund are able to put food on their family's table and rely on regular work. Perhaps then they can open up one of our Arabic Wikipedia pages to read about enlightenment values or learn how to start a business with proper support. These Innovation Hub grantees are pioneers who embrace their role as leaders to pursue a better future for their communities.

Our goal is clear: give the power back to the people, and prosperity will follow.

Faisal Al Mutar
President and Co-Founder
Ideas Beyond Borders

IDEAS BEYOND BORDERS

Remodeling development

[1] Sen, A. (1999). Development as Freedom. Oxford University Press.

The post-World War II era saw the establishment of an international development system aimed at rebuilding war-torn economies and promoting economic growth in less developed countries. This system, characterized by institutions like the World Bank and the International Monetary Fund, has been the primary mechanism for delivering aid and support to developing countries. However, as global challenges have evolved, the effectiveness and efficiency of this system have increasingly come under scrutiny. Critics argue that its top-down aid approach, bureaucratic inefficiencies, ingrained corruption, and lack of accountability have often led to suboptimal outcomes and, in some cases, exacerbated the very problems they sought to address.

As chaos continues to unfold across the Middle East, the current system has become even less viable due to a hesitancy to send funding to war-torn countries ruled by de facto regimes. And while that hesitancy might be understandable, that doesn't change the fact that the average citizen in these countries is hungry for a positive alternative. Given the opportunity, innovative individuals are poised to do the work to improve their societies, on their terms, armed with an intimate understanding of the local landscape. As the saying goes, "Give a man a fish, and you feed him for a day. Teach him how to fish, and you feed him for a lifetime."

Top-down approaches to development frequently prioritize the perspectives and priorities of donor countries or international organizations over the needs and knowledge of local communities. This disconnect can lead to the implementation of projects that are ill-suited to local conditions, resulting in limited impact and unsustainable outcomes. At Ideas Beyond Borders, we are equipping populations with the resources and skills necessary to become self-sufficient in the long term and reduce dependency upon external support. Effective development is dependent on gaining a deep understanding of the needs of the community, which requires meaningful engagement with people on the ground. Decisions made in board rooms by wealthy higher-ups too often lack the insights necessary to empower communities to support themselves once the aid well runs dry.

Embracing a more bottom-up, participatory method that prioritizes the voices and needs of local communities[1] strengthens accountability and transparency mechanisms, and integrates sustainability into the heart of the projects IBB supports and the people they impact. The complex, nuanced realities of communities living amidst extremism and hardship can only be addressed by those who understand the problem they are aiming to solve. Innovative solutions are essential to revitalizing the effectiveness of international aid.

INNOVATION HUB

We make quick decisions, minimizing bureaucracy.

We actively seek out unconventional thinkers who challenge norms.

We support projects that aim to benefit broader communities.

We foster a supportive community for collaboration and networking.

We back projects introducing new and transformative ideas in technology, social innovation, or addressing urgent challenges.

We have deep, on-the-ground knowledge of the Middle East, funding projects with consideration for barriers, cultural diversity, and geographical contexts.

We offer flexible funding tailored to project needs.

We embrace risk, encouraging ambitious projects.

Wheel Segments

- Fast Decision-Making
- Unconventional Thinking
- Community and Network Building
- Regional Insights
- Embracing Risk
- Flexible Funding
- Innovation at the Core
- Empowering Local Talent

INNOVATION HUB
مركز الابتكار
د نوښت مركز
ناوەندی داهێنان

3

[2] Cowen, Tyler. "The Great Stagnation: How America Ate All the Low-Hanging Fruit of Modern History, Got Sick, and Will (Eventually) Feel Better." Dutton, 2011. Cowen, Tyler. "Stubborn Attachments: A Vision for a Society of Free, Prosperous, and Responsible Individuals." Stripe Press, 2018. Acs, Zoltan J., et al. "Entrepreneurship, Economic Development, and Institutions." Small Business Economics, vol. 31, no. 3, 2008, pp. 219–234. Mazzucato, Mariana. "The Entrepreneurial State: Debunking Public vs. Private Sector Myths." Anthem Press, 2015. World Bank. "World Development Report 2020: Trading for Development in the Age of Global Value Chains." World Bank Publications, 2019.

Hence, the Innovation Hub model:

The Innovation Hub model, rooted in the emergent ventures theory popularized by economist Tyler Cowen, represents a departure from traditional top-down development approaches. Cowen's insights, particularly from his work in "The Great Stagnation" and "Stubborn Attachments," highlight the importance of nurturing organic, bottom-up innovation as a driver of economic growth and prosperity. Cowen argues that innovation is not a linear process driven solely by scientific breakthroughs or large-scale investment. Instead, he posits that much of the progress we've witnessed throughout history has been the result of countless small-scale innovations—what he terms "low-hanging fruit." By creating an environment conducive to experimentation and entrepreneurship, societies can unlock these latent sources of growth. The Innovation Hub model embodies this ethos by providing a platform for aspiring entrepreneurs to test their ideas, iterate on them, and ultimately scale them into viable businesses. By focusing on emergent ventures—those with the potential to disrupt existing markets or create entirely new ones—the model capitalizes on the dynamic nature of innovation. But what sets this approach apart is its emphasis on inclusivity and community empowerment. Unlike traditional development strategies that often rely on external expertise and resources, the Innovation Hub model seeks to leverage local talent and ingenuity.

Investing in homegrown solutions to local challenges not only fosters economic self-sufficiency but also strengthens social cohesion and resilience. The effectiveness of this approach is underscored by empirical evidence from various contexts. Studies have shown that grassroots entrepreneurship plays a crucial role in driving economic development, particularly in emerging economies where formal job opportunities may be scarce. Initiatives that share a similar model to the Innovation Hub have catalyzed significant economic growth and poverty reduction by providing aspiring entrepreneurs access to seed or growth funding. Moreover, these initiatives contribute to long-lasting positive progress by prioritizing employment generation and local value creation. The Innovation Hub model represents a paradigm shift in how we approach economic development. The model promotes sustainability by equipping local populations with the skills and resources necessary to manage their development trajectory independently. Embracing this change requires rethinking the structure and goals of development programs and implementing robust accountability measures to mitigate corruption and inefficiency. As we move forward, it is crucial to integrate these more dynamic, bottom-up approaches to overcome bureaucratic inertia and corruption. This approach represents a critical step towards a more effective and equitable development system that genuinely serves the needs of the world's most vulnerable populations.

Embracing the principles of emergent ventures theory[2] and coupling them with a commitment to inclusivity and community empowerment offers a more holistic and sustainable pathway to prosperity. By supporting local entrepreneurs and community projects, the Innovation Hub not only addresses immediate economic needs but also builds a resilient foundation for future development. This model ensures that development efforts are both adap-

INNOVATION HUB

> *"Every startup needs an angel's push at some point and that's exactly how it felt with Ideas Beyond Borders. I now know that in the future when I have the means I'll be supporting upcoming startups the same way."*
>
> **Natheer Halawani**
> Entrepreneur

Natheer Halawani is promoting a culture of cycling in the Lebanese city of Tripoli

tive to the nuanced realities of each community and robust against the inefficiencies and corruption that have plagued conventional methods. As we pivot to this innovative future, we embrace a development strategy that genuinely supports and uplifts the world's most vulnerable populations, paving the way for a more prosperous global society. This resilience-building aspect of the Innovation Hub model instills a sense of hope, showing that even in the face of adversity, communities can thrive.

Reid Newton
Lead Editor of Ideas Beyond Borders

IDEAS BEYOND BORDERS

The Innovation Hub in action

What if Afghan women could study and earn, despite the education ban? Or work as journalists and tell the truth about life under the Taliban? How might an arts club inspire hope among marginalized youth in southern Iraq? And could a cycling club change the lives of girls in Baghdad? There is only one way to find out.

In 2021, Ideas Beyond Borders pilot-tested a program to provide small grants to ordinary people with bold ideas. Proposals flooded in from across the Middle East and Afghanistan with creative solutions to ongoing problems—secret schools for girls in Kabul, tech skills for unemployed youth in Lebanon, support for startups in Kurdistan, free speech via a pioneering book club in Karbala, Iraq.

Since then, we have funded over 200 projects, reaching people in Iraq, Kurdistan, Lebanon, Iran, Jordan, Turkey, Syria, Egypt, and Afghanistan. Results are gradual at first, but then lives start to change—young people get jobs, talent finds an outlet for expression, and women see a glimmer of opportunity when they thought all was lost.

This book is about the progress that's possible as a new generation of innovators steps forward across the Arab world. But without support, populations faced with conflict, corruption, economic collapse, instability, and the oppressive rule of authoritarian regimes lose hope in their homelands. Our aim at Ideas Beyond Borders is to help them bring it back.

Bold ideas with lasting impact

Before the Arab Spring, around ten to twelve percent of the region's youth emigrated abroad. Now, more than half of young Arabs in North Africa and the Levant want to emigrate, according to Asda'a BCW's 2023 Arab Youth Survey, with economic

"With Ideas Beyond Borders' assistance, we could cover internet costs and provide effective mentorship to our students. Consequently, many of our graduates have secured remote job opportunities and are now employed as software developers."

Ahmad Zia Yousufi
Head of the "Kick-Start to Software Development" project in Afghanistan

instability and the lack of job opportunities among the most commonly cited causes of brain drain in Arab countries. The situation only gets worse as violence, war, and the oppressive rule of authoritarian regimes force more people to flee, often via dangerous routes to nations hostile to their presence.

For many, there is no choice—survival depends on leaving. Others refuse to relinquish the dream of a better life at home. They are determined to channel their skills and creativity into improving the outlook of their countries so that people with diverse talents and interests can thrive there once more. Our mission at Ideas Beyond Borders is to find these people and empower them to transform ideas into actions, reshaping towns and cities so that new generations can discover their potential, invest in their environments, and see the results of their labor grow.

Change starts small, in local communities where an idea takes shape. Plans are made, support is gathered, and hope begins to spread. In Sulaymaniyah, a young man sees friends struggling to find work. He starts Wedonet, a network that connects local talent with employers, giving people a chance to launch their careers and bolster the creative sector in southern Kurdistan. In Lebanon, a coding school called SE Factory runs programming courses for unemployed youth, giving them skills to access tech jobs online. And in Afghanistan, where women and girls face an uncertain future, a teacher runs secret schools behind closed doors, educating female students in defiance of the ruling Taliban regime.

These solutions have the potential to substantially change the future, and the Innovation Hub helps them succeed. Ideas Beyond Borders supports hundreds of change-makers burning with creative, cultural, and educational ideas through this program. These are their responses to problems they know—solutions forged in struggles seen and heard by people determined to make a difference.

Empowering the right people

Above all, Innovation Hub grants are accessible, so no one is shut out. We provide easy-access microloans for small projects with the capacity to make a real difference—a tailored approach designed by people on the ground.

Our team has extensive local knowledge and a vast network across the region, but we don't claim to be experts in every community across the Arab world. Only those who have lived in a particular Iraqi town or Afghan village can appreciate its unique social fabric and how traditions and beliefs have shaped it over time. So, when it comes to addressing the

Female taxi service Lygo allows women to travel independently around Mosul so they can get to school, university and work. Image: Osama Al Maqdoni

issues confronting these communities, we defer to the expertise of local innovators in devising solutions that truly serve their societies.

People like Hakam Hesham Abed, who launched Lygo, a new taxi service staffed by female drivers to improve freedom of movement for women in Mosul, Iraq. "If a woman doesn't have a car, or one of her male relatives doesn't, she cannot go anywhere," Abed told us. An Innovation Hub grant enabled him to create the Lygo app so women won't have to miss university classes or relinquish job offers because they lack access to transportation.

It's a small change with the capacity to make a crucial impact—another barrier standing in the way of meaningful progress broken down. And if a project doesn't succeed, because even good ideas fail, this is still money well spent because more than the project or business, it's the person behind the idea whose passion and determination will drive them to try again and again.

Confronting challenges head-on

That's why we supported Kamaran Safar, who tried multiple businesses before launching his leather goods brand in Kurdistan. His aim is to train 1,000 stay-at-home mothers to make beautiful bags, wallets, and laptop cases so they can start their own businesses and secure an independent income.

Hero Junior Academy educates street children in Afghanistan, running classes in the morning before they go out to work. Image: Paeez Jahanbin

As a petroleum engineer, he could have self-funded the startup over time, but instead he limited his investment and applied for funding to show other young changemakers what is possible. "I have survived the setbacks because I want to make change through business and inspire other Kurdish youth to do the same," he says. "We can do business for profit, but why not use it for social change too?"

This is the thinking that inspires our faith in a better future and shows how longstanding challenges can be overcome. It is where impoverished women find work with a Beirut boutique, a bookshop brings culture to war-torn Sinjar, and street children in Afghanistan are educated free of charge.

School teacher Ahmad Jawid Karimyan has already launched libraries in rural areas across Afghanistan. Now he wants to show children who work as shoe shiners or beggars that life can be more than basic survival through his school, Hero Junior Academy. "When I go there and see their faces, their enthusiasm to learn or study, their progress, it compels me to work harder for them," he says.

Targeted support

These ideas push past the rhetoric of corrupt governments and foreign agendas to serve sidelined populations whose voices are largely unheard. For many of our grantees, development funding is beyond reach, reserved for those with the contacts and leverage to secure large grants.

The Innovation Hub is a rebuttal to this top-down system—a way to cut through corruption, bypass bureaucracy, and empower everyday people to pursue positive change. "I suddenly realized that this was the program that should have existed years ago; maybe then it wouldn't have felt so hopeless to daydream about a better future for our country and the rest of the Middle East," says Faisal Al Mutar, President of Ideas Beyond Borders.

Today, we are working to restore that hope, project by project, person by person, to communities across the Middle East and Afghanistan. This book explores how ideas were born and nurtured in the minds of those who inspired us to share their dedication and belief. The Innovation Hub is our investment in their future, a way of helping them flourish so that ideas can grow and spread, rippling outwards to inform a new generation, who one day soon will reshape the region.

INNOVATION HUB

> "I have a deep belief in free thought and believe that new interactivemedia platforms are one of the most important tools to achieve this."

Osama Essa
Founder of Shezomedia in Jordan, one of IBB's first Innovation Hub grantees

• IRAQ

Iraq

Re-writing the future in Iraq

In early 2007, when the Iraq war was at its height, a report predicted the toll it would take on future generations. Living in streets stalked by gunmen, where car bombs and kidnappings were a constant threat, was having a profound impact on Iraqi children. Many had learning impediments brought on by living in a climate of insecurity and some were found to be suffering from extreme stress. The report, by the Association of Iraqi Psychologists, cited parents who were afraid to let their children leave the house, even to go to school.

Two decades later, these young people have never known their country at peace. The brutal oppression of Saddam Hussein's rule gave way to the endless bloodshed of the US-led invasion in 2003, with outbreaks of internecine conflict and violent extremism in the years since. Then came the chilling brutality of the ISIS occupation in 2014, followed by the proliferation of lawless militias who operate with impunity, fuelling fear and insecurity on Iraq's streets.

In this febrile climate, activists are murdered for participating in protests, and influencers go missing after expressing their views in a tweet. Journalists are silenced and academics assassinated by shadowy groups, many with links to Iran. Despite these dangers, tens of thousands of Iraqis joined the Tishreen Protests in October 2019, facing military-grade tear gas and live ammunition to call for an end to corruption and the overthrow of the regime.

Breaking barriers

At the heart of these protests were young people seeking job opportunities, many of them university graduates unable to find work. "My generation lives with the idea that they have a lot of potential but no means to achieve it," says Rafal Al Adilee, MENA project manager at Ideas Beyond Borders. "Iraq is filled with talented people, but a poor education system, political instability, and violent unrest have blocked them from realizing their dreams."

Basra Old City with Al Sayyab Statue by Iraqi artist Neshaat Al Shammari

INNOVATION HUB

IRAQ

When Al Adilee, 30, joined IBB in 2022, she set about mitigating these circumstances by giving a new generation the chance to achieve their goals. Prioritizing people who add value to their communities, she sought out sustainable projects with the capacity to make a lasting impact and inspire others to do the same. "Through this program, we have offered opportunities to dozens of talented people who struggle to find funding elsewhere. We want to help people pursue creative ideas that improve their environments," Al Adilee says.

She focuses on spreading knowledge, skills, and experience by funding projects that promote economic independence, create jobs, and foster the private sector in Iraq. Through the Innovation Hub, she is helping young Iraqis put talent into practice and pursue their goals where that has long seemed impossible. "By removing the barriers, we can encourage young people to invest their energies in transformative ideas rather than seeking the first job they can get with a stable income," she adds.

Legacy of learning

Growing up in different provinces across the country, Al Adilee experienced a cross-section of Iraqi society and believes the country's diversity is exactly why innovation can thrive. While recent decades have sown division along religious and ethnic lines, older Iraqis remember periods of greater harmony when Muslim, Christian, and Jewish children played together, and the country's Arab, Kurdish, Yazidi, Assyrian, Turkmen, and other communities lived side by side.

These days, sectarian struggles simmer at the surface, fuelled by powerful actors who inflame tensions to suit political ends. But beneath these artificial fractures is a society built on myriad cultures whose heritage draws on influences that stretch from East to West.

One particular era encapsulates this breadth, when Baghdad was a melting pot of cultures as people came from across the empire to participate in its success. This period, from the eighth century until 1258, was known as the Islamic Golden Age, when the Abbasid caliphs amassed books from across the empire to fill great libraries, fuel scientific inquiry, and harness the knowledge of the ancient world. In the center of their new capital, Baghdad, they built the House of Wisdom and embarked on a major movement to translate the works of the Greeks and other civilizations into Arabic.

This was the inspiration behind Bayt Al Hikma 2.0, Ideas Beyond Borders' flagship translation project, which aims to be a contemporary online version of the renowned Abbasid academy. "The golden age was a time when freedom of expression flourished in the Arab world," says Faisal al Mutar, President of Ideas Beyond Borders. "By making works of science and culture available in Arabic, and translating ideas into action through the Innovation Hub, we are drawing on the legacy of this era, when the

"My generation lives with the idea that they have a lot of potential but no means to achieve it. Iraq is filled with talented people, but a poor education system, political instability, and violent unrest have blocked them from realizing their dreams."

Rafal Al Adilee
MENA project manager
at Ideas Beyond Borders

pursuit of knowledge and enterprise was prized above all else."

Drawing on the past

It's a legacy that Iraqi artist Neshaat Al Shammari celebrates in his paintings of Abbasid architecture, reminding people of a time when Baghdad was at the center of science and learning. With support from an Innovation Hub grant, he has created digital resources to educate and inspire people curious about this great academic age. "These people amassed a huge amount of knowledge; it's important to tell their stories. "It's about bringing it alive and making it relevant for the modern day," he says.

His pieces capture the spirit of this pioneering time and reinforce the power of art and culture to shape the future. It's why Ideas Beyond Borders uses the Innovation Hub to empower young creatives in the Middle East and Afghanistan, from photographers and painters who celebrate their heritage to digital designers and jewelry makers using their talents to educate society, embrace progress and inspire belief in opportunities for change.

Almost five years after massive demonstrations brought central Baghdad to a standstill, the roads around Tahrir Square still tell the story of the protests that began in October 2019. Walls daubed in murals capture the desperation that drove thousands to the streets, calling for an end to corruption, unemployment, and poor public services. The images capture the solidarity of that time as people of all faiths and backgrounds marched side by side, despite a violent crackdown by security forces that killed more than 600 people and injured over 20,000 in the first six months.

It's a potent representation of art's role in revolution and the issues it gives voice to. But too often, artists and other innovators lack the resources to achieve their goals. That's when the Innovation Hub steps in, bypassing the cronyism of traditional funding networks to reach those with a genuine desire to achieve lasting change. "The solution has to come from the people. Making it easier for individuals who have good ideas to get funding is the way to make this happen. We are just a catalyst," Al Mutar says.

A fresh outlook

Providing opportunities where they have long been denied is enriching work, and Ideas Beyond Borders is only just beginning. The more time we spend with aspiring innovators, the better we understand their needs. This increasingly includes support for start-ups and entrepreneurs as a new generation steps forward to drive the development of an emerging small business scene.

"Working on the Innovation Hub has given me an excellent insight into what matters most," says Al Adilee, who met digital artist Jaafar Alsaadi during the 2019 uprising. His prints, depicting the courage and sacrifice of those heady days, laid the foundations for XO Center, the online platform he launched in 2022 to help young artists raise their profile, sell work, and connect with potential clients online. "It's a shortcut for them to start their careers," explains Alsaadi, who recently re-launched the website following a re-design funded by Ideas Beyond Borders. "So many people here have the talent, but there's no support to present their work."

Iraq remains a problematic environment for startups. Bureaucratic hurdles, corruption, limited access to funding, and wider social, economic, and political challenges create impossible conditions for many entrepreneurs. But between these barriers, a few find opportunities and persevere against the odds to prove that it is possible to succeed. These are the people that the Innovation Hub supports, who persevere to make a difference. For these young innovators, the challenges are a reason to try harder because there is opportunity on the other side. As Alsaadi says, "Iraq is the best place to start something fresh because, whatever you do, it's exciting and new."

IRAQ

*Images:
Osama Al Maqdoni.*

Driving change: Lygo is shifting gears with a women-only taxi service

Lygo is empowering women in Mosul by providing them with safe and socially acceptable transportation

At first, it was difficult to find female taxi drivers in Mosul. Many families in Iraq's conservative second city do not allow women to work, let alone as drivers. But in the past few months, female-driven taxis have become a familiar sight, ferrying women to university in the morning or collecting them from work in the afternoons, addressing a glaring gap in transport options for half the city's population.

"It's a revolutionary idea," says Hakam Hesham, who last year launched Lygo, a taxi service staffed by female drivers, which he hopes will transform travel and improve freedom of movement for women in Mosul.

He has witnessed first-hand the frustration felt by women forced to forgo education and employment opportunities because they lack transportation. Ride-hailing companies like Uber, Bolt and Careem don't operate in Mosul, and there's no public transport in the city. "If a woman doesn't have a car, or one of her male relatives doesn't, she cannot go anywhere," Hesham explains.

The idea came to him after his friend failed to show up to a hackathon. "She said there was nobody to take her there, and she couldn't use a taxi because females cannot share a car with men they do not know," he says. His plan is to open the city up to women as it embraces a new era after the trauma of the ISIS occupation between 2014 and 2017.

Since the destructive nine-month battle to expel ISIS from Mosul, recovery has been slow, but there are signs of progress that fill Hesham with hope. Reconstruction is finally moving forward, including on the city's airport, signaling an intention to open up to the world once again. "Optimism is everywhere, we now have big events attended by singers and artists from all over the country," Hesham says.

Demand has been consistently high since he launched Lygo, and he is already eyeing expansion. Most mornings and afternoons, his taxis are fully booked, primarily by university students traveling to and from class. "At the moment, demand is much greater than supply. We get tons of calls," he says.

Unlike regular taxis, Lygo enables women to book from home so they don't have to wait on the street. It also affords a sense of security for women who prefer traveling with a female driver. "It's more socially acceptable, safe, and convenient," Hesham explains.

Not everyone supports the idea. There has been pushback from male taxi drivers who feel threatened by the new competition. "They have started spreading rumors, saying that these women can't drive and they will cause accidents and problems," says Hesham. A few men even started creating fake profiles and placing bogus orders to disrupt their service.

Mostly, though, there has also been a lot of support, particularly from the women of Mosul, as well as human rights activists and organizations, including Ideas Beyond Borders, which provided an Innovation Hub grant to fund the creation of a Lygo app.

The next step, says Hesham, is to expand the fleet and become the official airport taxi for female travelers. At present, most of their customers are local, but Hesham is confident that the transformation taking place in Mosul will encourage more people to visit the city, and when they do, his female drivers will be waiting to collect them.

> *"At the moment demand is much greater than supply. We get tons of calls."*
>
> **Hakam Hesham**
> Founder of Lygo

◉ IRAQ

Harmony in the midst of hardship: Reviving Basra's cultural legacy through the arts

Ali Elmadanie hopes to reclaim Basra as Iraq's cultural capital and restore hope to a jaded population

Ali Elmadanie, founder of Jummarts

Lining up on the street, Ali Elmadanie could feel his heart pounding as people moved into position. It was evening time, and passersby were pausing, curious at this unusual display. Afterwards, he would say it felt exhilarating, empowering, to lose themselves in the sound of the music, as they performed en masse in the southern Iraqi city of Basra.

"People were amazed, but nobody tried to stop us. Maybe some onlookers didn't approve, but they didn't say anything," says Elmadanie, who organizes theatre and music performances in Basra through his arts organization Jummarts.

His aim is to support aspiring artists and revive the conservative city's faded reputation as Iraq's cultural capital. "We want to get people accustomed to seeing arts again—remind them that it's part of their identity," he adds.

Basra is a long way from the place that birthed some of Iraq's most famous musicians and once hosted major poetry competitions. Today, the city is better known for its oil and gas reserves; a would-be boomtown, where half-completed construction projects loom over slums that stand in stark contrast to the huge houses owned by a small elite that harbors its natural wealth.

In the past, Basra looked set to become another Dubai, but its vast concentration of crude reserves has done little to dispel the poverty of a province mired in corruption. Instead, decades of conflict have sown division and discontent, presided over by powerful militias who rule through intimidation. "After successive wars, people have lost interest in arts," Elmadanie says.

Jummarts is trying to revive that interest and restore Basra's identity as a place where the arts can flourish. With help from an Ideas Beyond Borders Innovation Hub grant, the team has moved to a larger premises and purchased new equipment to expand operations and reach more people. "We are trying to make society more inclusive and in harmony with itself. That way people can live freely, safely and at peace," Elmadanie says.

Before the fighting that fractured its community, Basra was a place where people of all ethnicities mingled and worked. As Iraq's only seaport, it welcomed travelers from around the world, absorbing the different cultural influences they brought with them.

"If we go back a few decades, not even that far, Iraqi society was living in harmony," Elmadanie says. "Music and art remind people of the things they have in common—the more people focus on the arts, the more they will dwell on the beautiful things that make them human and one single community."

This is a vision he shares with Ideas Beyond Borders. "Listening to a Jummarts musical performance reminds us of another Iraq, with a rich culture and a history of creativity," says Faisal Al Mutar, President of Ideas Beyond Borders. "It's by supporting enterprises like this that we come closer to this Iraq and the opportunities it offers for a generation eager to invest their talents."

Many of the musical instruments that come from Iraq were invented in Basra, like the Khashaba, a narrow hand-held drum made of wood. Anyone familiar with the country's musical tradition knows the distinctive sound of the Khashaba, but playing it is difficult. "It's a more specialized instrument; it doesn't play notes," explains Elmadanie, who runs classes in traditional Iraqi instruments like the Khashaba and the Darbouke to prevent these skills from dying out.

Between lessons, Elmadanie and the Jummarts troupe of musicians and actors perform at restaurants and hotels, playing music and putting on plays. Elmadanie earns enough to make a living from this work, which is rare in Iraq. "We have a saying that arts will not put food on your table," he says. Jummarts is trying to change that by giving people the chance to develop their talent while creating a more hospitable environment for artists in Basra.

The interest is there, he says, but a few people run all the art activities in the city, and access can be tricky. "It's a consortium of a very few organizations, and they are not inclusive. That's the difference I'm trying to make."

Growing up in one of the city's poorest neighborhoods, he worked hard to gain a degree in engineering but found an outlet for his creativity in theater, attending workshops and participating in performances before moving on to writing and directing plays. Jummarts came from his desire to share this passion with more people and invite everyone to take part, particularly people with disabilities who have few opportunities to participate in Basra's small creative sector.

"Before the arts, I used to see the world with my eyes. Now I see the world with everybody's eyes," Elmadanie says.

He dreams of a time when Basra is not synonymous with conflict and oppression, or the oil that has been more of a blight than a blessing for the city's sidelined population. In reviving Basra's cultural legacy, he hopes to reclaim its scattered soul and bring hope to a population weary of struggle. "When you go on Google and search the name of any Iraqi city, the pictures show explosions and destruction. I want people to search Basra and see something positive in the results, like our performances."

⬤ IRAQ

Peddling equality

Suad El Gohary is inspiring Iraqi women to ride their bikes and show the next generation that cycling is not just a sport for men

It's rare to see a woman riding a bicycle in Baghdad, so when Suad El Gohary pedals past a fellow female cyclist, she marks the moment with a wave. These days, she no longer feels like the only woman riding a bike around Iraq's capital city, largely thanks to the cycling group she created, which is pushing back against conservative cultural norms to carve out space for female cyclists in Iraq.

"Many women want to cycle but are forbidden by their families. We have one woman who came in secret with her daughters because her husband wouldn't allow it," says El Gohary, 53. Her ambition is to change this by empowering women to ride their bicycles freely through the streets of Baghdad and other Iraqi cities. In time, she hopes a new generation will see it as a normal part of everyday life.

So far, there have been small but promising signs of change. "It's still rare, but nowadays I do encounter other women cycling around," says El Gohary, who founded the Palm Watan cycling team during the pandemic when the lockdown imposed strict limits on pedestrians and cars. "Cycling became really popular in Baghdad after Covid. There are lots of men who get together and ride for fun, but ours is the only female group," she adds.

El Gohary works as a journalist, covering social and political issues for Iraqi media. Her profile and network have helped her gain traction for the team, which is gathering support across the country as more Iraqi women embrace the opportunity to ride a bike. "I'm now seeing females in other cities who want to ride their bikes with us—in Kirkuk, Basra, Diyala—they are asking us to expand to their regions," El Gohary says.

Female cyclists are considered controversial in Iraq, where many feel it flouts strict social codes. For

IDEAS BEYOND BORDERS INNOVATION HUB

some, the image of a woman riding a bicycle is a flagrant violation of behavioral norms, and El Gohary has at times been harassed for riding her bike. "I'm always a bit worried on my bike because men look at me in a very weird, sometimes aggressive way," she says.

Not long ago, she sustained a serious eye injury after a man attacked her in the street for riding her bicycle. But she refuses to be cowed. For her, cycling has been transformative, and she wants to share the freedom and health benefits of riding a bike with women across Iraq.

"After suffering from joint pain for years, the doctor advised me to take up exercise. I tried the bike, and I loved it. I became a happier, healthier person," she says. But it was during the pandemic that she decided to encourage more women to try it out. At the time, Baghdad was under lockdown with a curfew in place, and people were struggling to get hold of daily necessities.

"I started contacting women that I know and offering to buy their groceries and bring them on my bike," says El Gohary. This soon inspired other women, so she started teaching them to cycle, and they quickly became a team. Now, they are training children—both boys and girls—how to ride bikes and supporting them to compete in national events. Ultimately, she hopes to change the culture around cycling in Iraq and encourage a new generation to embrace the sport.

With support from an Ideas Beyond Borders Innovation Hub grant, she plans to expand their activities to Mosul and teach children there how to ride a bike. The grant also covers the purchase of new bicycles so they can practice and then participate in races in the future. "We're trying to create a connection between these young boys and girls so that when they grow up, men will look at them more as equals because they trained together as kids."

She visited Mosul in 2022 to witness the city's first all-female cycling marathon. Friends wanted her to rest as she recovered from eye surgery following the attack, but she is determined to keep going. "Things are starting to change. I can't let the momentum die down," she says.

Image: Osama Al Maqdoni.

> *"Many women want to cycle but are forbidden by their families. We have one woman who came in secret with her daughters because her husband wouldn't allow it."*
>
> **Suad El Gohary**
> Founder of the
> Palm Watan Cycling team

Suad El Gohary is inspiring a movement of female cyclists in Iraq

◆ IRAQ

Free speech in one of Iraq's most conservative cities

A book club in Karbala is carving out space for free speech among those who have been warned to stay silent

Mohammed Gelewkhan was 14 when he was warned against asking questions in class. A voracious reader, he was curious to know more about Iraqi society and its relationship with religion. He was accused of atheism, a serious allegation in Iraq, and told to stay silent. "It taught me not to speak openly in society; you really have to be careful where you speak," says Gelewkhan.

These days, he reserves probing questions for Enki, a book club that provides rare opportunities for discussion and debate in his home city, Karbala, a holy place for Shia Muslims in Iraq. "It's lovely to have a place like Enki to talk openly—anywhere else things would go wrong," says Gelewkhan, now just 16 years old.

Earlier this year, he attended the club's session on *Rationality* by Canadian cognitive psychologist Steven Pinker, whose works have been translated into Arabic by Ideas Beyond Borders. Over 40 people showed up to discuss the book, which affirms the human capacity for clear reasoning and examines the tools we use to get there. It is a textbook on critical thinking, rejecting claims that humans are inherently irrational beings, pointing to the power of logic and reasoning over illusions like bigotry and bias.

This was fertile ground for Enki attendees, who examined the spread of pseudo-science, the rationality of religious belief, and the nature of morality, particularly in the Abrahamic faiths. The session ran over, lasting more than two hours. "People were deep in discussion, drawing connections between the themes in Pinker's book and real life in the Middle East," says Hameed Majeed Hameed, who founded the book club in 2022.

"Reading this book can change the way people perceive information and help them differentiate between information and misinformation," he adds, pointing to the power of local religious leaders to steer public opinion in Karbala.

Growing up here, Hameed felt the need to carve out space for free expression, somewhere beyond the reach of strict social constraints. Life in the conservative city can feel stifling, particularly for younger generations. So, he teamed up with fellow students to launch Enki, naming it after the Sumerian god of wisdom to reinforce the power of books and education.

More than 400 people applied to attend the first session as men and women embraced the rare opportunity to discuss scientific subjects and engage in open debate. "Karbala is so conservative that even people studying physics at university hardly discuss science. All they talk about is religion," says Hameed, who studies law at the University of Karbala.

Enki participants now gather regularly to explore a range of books covering philosophy, science, psychology, and other fields, from Charles Darwin's *On the Origin of the Species* to works by Richard Dawkins. Many are students like Hameed, though they encourage everyone to attend, hoping to open people's minds to new ideas and broaden their thinking in a free and friendly debate environment.

Mohammed recalls one surprising afternoon when his father arrived early to pick him up and decided to join in. "It was really fun and refreshing seeing my dad, an older—not very liberal—conservative Iraqi man, talking about his views with youth who have different ideas," he says.

While Mohammed's parents appreciate his passion for reading, they don't share his appetite for philosophy and science. "They just don't really take it seriously; they see philosophy as this weird witchery that people engage in to complicate their lives," he says. Denied a receptive outlet at school and at home, Enki is a lifeline for his intellectual curiosity, a place to interact with like-minded people who share his desire to learn.

Last year, Enki secured an Innovation Hub grant to run more gatherings, moving from fortnightly to weekly sessions to meet mounting demand. Hameed sees these sessions as a starting point for young people pushing back against the free speech gatekeepers in Karbala, but there's a long way to go. He cites the fate of Karbala's contemporary art gallery, The Salah Hithani Museum, as an example of the hostility towards new cultural movements in the city. "Initially, we held our sessions there, but local leaders had it closed. They saw the gallery as a threat to the holiness of the city, so now it's a video gaming hall," he says.

Hameed does not exaggerate the scope of a single book club to change the status quo. Books alone cannot alter the course of history, but if enough people join the discussion, he believes perspectives will shift. Since the Tishreen protests of 2019, when tens of thousands took to Iraq's streets, there has been a new receptiveness to ideas among many Iraqi youth.

"Things like this really move the mindset of young people in Iraq. Sadly, you can't really change the older adults; their conservatism is baked in, but youth mentality is certainly better than before," adds Mohammed, who attends most weeks. The sessions have restored his confidence since that frightening experience at school and allowed him to believe that one day, it may be less dangerous to express opinions in public. "Judging by my relatives and classmates, the future doesn't inspire me, but seeing how people at Enki engage with philosophy and science fills me with hope. It makes me happy, and I feel a bit more safe when I look around the

> *"Reading this book can change the way people perceive information and help them differentiate between information and misinformation."*
>
> **Hameed Majeed Hameed**
> Founder of Enki Club

IRAQ

room at people engaging in open discussion," he says.

Not everyone who attends is a literary enthusiast. Zaher Jamal, a 21-year-old civil engineering student, has little time for extra-curricular reading, but something about Enki piqued his curiosity. "It gave me that space for books. I love seeing people discuss issues with open minds. There's a real sense of community," he says. Attending the discussion on *Rationality*, he was struck by the frankness of the debate on topics that would be off-limits elsewhere.

"I never imagined being able to influence and be influenced by others; it's really beneficial. Since joining Enki, I'm reading more and sharing these ideas with certain friends and members of my family," he says.

This is the gradual influence that Hameed hopes for when he imagines the impact of Enki in the months and years ahead. On several occasions, he has overheard strangers mirroring conversations from book club sessions, proof, he hopes, that ideas are spreading. "If enough people read a book, it inspires dialogue and debate. A club like Enki can ignite those discussions and, maybe one day, that can lead to change," he says.

Enki participants gather regularly to discuss books on philosophy, science, psychology, and other fields

Iraq in print: The entrepreneur behind Baghdad's digital art craze

XO Center is at the heart of a burgeoning art scene that's giving artists and designers a new way to showcase and sell their work online

Jaafar Alsaadi is at the forefront of Iraq's burgeoning entrepreneurial scene

"Iraq is the best place to start something because whatever you do, it's new," says Jaafar Alsaadi, the founder of a digital printing platform in Baghdad. That's true for the 22-year-old, who set up XO Center in 2022 to create a new space for Iraqi artists and designers to sell their work online. His T-shirts, hoodies and tote bags are now a familiar sight around the city, featuring original prints by artists and designers from across Iraq and the wider Middle East.

"So many people here have the talent, but there's no support to present their work," says Alsaadi, who works with artists to develop their designs for the commercial market. "We help them make the design successful."

When he first pitched the idea to startup advisors at The Station, a coworking space and incubator in Baghdad, he had no idea it would catch on so fast. As a teenager, he used to get the album covers of American rock band Evanescence printed into posters and distribute them among friends. Then, during the Tishreen protests that gripped Iraq in 2019, he started printing revolution art, eventually creating a website to display the work for potential buyers. The concept grew from there.

The platform became the XO Center interface, providing a dashboard for artists and designers to develop their brand and showcase their work while building a client base across the region. "It's a shortcut for them to start their careers," explains Alsaadi, who re-launched the website following a re-design funded by an Innovation Hub grant from Ideas Beyond Borders.

📍 IRAQ

XO Center is a platform for digital artists in Iraq to showcase and sell their work

It's a good industry to be in for young Iraqis, who face high unemployment rates, particularly among youth, with 36 percent currently out of work. "The future is digital art and graphic design. This is where the market is; your work can be implemented thousands of times," explains Alsaadi, who has helped more than 50 artists and designers secure jobs in Iraq. "Companies are always contacting me with roles they want to fill—graphic designers, animators, digital artists, graphic designers—there's lots of demand," he says.

XO Center doesn't own the rights to the work it prints. The artists are free to sell it wherever they choose. Instead, Alsaadi uses the majority of the sale proceeds to cover the price of the products and printing costs, setting aside 20 percent to ensure the artists receive a commission. "It's impossible to give them more than this and cover the costs unless we price higher, but that's not realistic in this market," he says.

Prices range from a few dollars for printed mugs and pencils, to $18 for a T-shirt, $20 for a hoodie, and $60 for a large poster on a wooden base.

Sourcing these products, at the quality XO Center requires, is challenging, particularly in Iraq. Shipping raw materials from Jordan is too expensive, so now he's speaking with suppliers in Turkey. "A lot of people try to con you; they send you a good sample and then poor products after that."

But he's not deterred by these challenges. Alsaadi is rapidly conquering the market for digital printing in Iraq and recently launched a sister company to provide BTB printing services for clients, including the regional ride-hailing giant Careem and international toothpaste brand Signal. "We don't have the same opportunities as places like Dubai, so when you do something new people get excited," he says.

Already, he has inspired numerous other small startups, expanding the pool of platforms for Iraqi designers while helping the industry grow. "Entrepreneurs like Jaafar are reframing the future of Iraq. We're relying on this energy and innovation to build businesses into flourishing sectors that can support a new generation of Iraqis with the appetite to make their country work," says Faisal Al Mutar, President of Ideas Beyond Borders.

The next step for XO Center will be a physical space, where designers and artists can display their work in different contexts. Alsaadi hopes this will help them reach diverse audiences, and, in doing so, offer alternative perspectives on Iraq, both at home and abroad. "Our designers are trying to make an identity for Iraq, make it alive again," he says. "They are exploring our history, culture, and traditions to present Iraq in a better light for the people and the world."

◆ IRAQ

Solar power: Surviving summer in Iraq

As power cuts make life miserable in Mosul, people are switching to solar panels to manage the searing summer heat

Images: Osama Al Maqdoni

By late August, life in Mosul feels relentless. Where possible, people stay indoors, blinds drawn against the sun's fierce blaze. Every few hours, the electricity comes on, and fans creak into gear, temporarily dissipating the thick wall of heat. Those with air-con enjoy the wash of cold air, but only for a few hours. Then the power goes off again.

Iraq has faced several summers of extreme heat in recent years. Last August, people in Basra saw temperatures climb above 51C, making it the hottest city in the world that week, while several other provinces suffered similar spikes. Heightened demand on the ailing national grid fuels frequent power outages, leaving Iraqis with little respite from months of melting heat.

Weathering the crisis

In the northern city of Mosul, the situation is particularly acute, partly due to the destruction of vital infrastructure during the fight to expel ISIS. Residents here contend with some of Iraq's worst electricity shortages, forcing those who can afford it to rely on expensive private generators, which cost around $60 to supply an average home. Everyone else has to put up with food spoiling in warm fridges, stifling summer days and sleepless nights. In temperatures like these, life quickly becomes intolerable.

But hope comes in the form of solar panels, offering a quiet, clean alternative to fill the energy void. In recent years, they have become a familiar sight on public buildings and private rooftops across the city as more residents invest in an energy supply that relies on something Iraq has in abundance—sunshine. "It's spreading rapidly in Mosul; even the streetlights have solar panels," says Mustafa Almola, who runs a solar power start-up in Mosul.

The trend began in towns and villages outside the city as international NGOs introduced solar panels to provide Iraqi farmers with power to run their equipment. As interest spread to the city, Almola spotted a business opportunity. In 2021 he launched Megawatt Solar to improve access to electricity and offer a cleaner supply. Now he is looking to expand to other parts of Iraq amid rising demand.

"People are happy with solar power. The units really improve their quality of life. With fewer generators around, the air is cleaner, the electricity bill is smaller, and people are able to withstand the summer," he says.

Bribes at the border

At first glance, Iraq appears to be one of the most energy-rich countries in the world, with the fifth-largest crude oil and twelfth-largest natural gas reserves, second only to Saudi Arabia among OPEC's top oil producers. Despite this, Iraq still imports around a third of its power needs from Iran, leaving it vulnerable to the kind of geopolitical maneuvering that resulted in acute outages when Iranian supplies were cut during a dispute over sanctions waivers in July 2023.

Frustration at the regular power outages, particularly in a country with such massive hydrocarbon reserves, reaches boiling point with increasing frequency. Protests have become a regular feature of Iraqi summers, as people vent their fury at the pervasive corruption and mismanagement that perpetuates the country's power crisis. "The situation is miserable in Iraq; people are without electricity, so they protest in the streets," says Almola. "If it wasn't for the generators and the solar panels being installed, they wouldn't be able to survive the summer."

Despite the urgent need for reform, little progress has been made in improving the country's energy infrastructure and addressing the issues that undermine supply. Meanwhile, population growth and the impacts of climate change place mounting pressure on the dilapidated grid. Iraq is considered the fifth-most-vulnerable country to the impacts of climate change globally, with soaring temperatures, drought, floods and other impacts undermining supply just as demand rockets each year.

In June 2023, Iraq's electricity ministry announced that power generation stood at 24,000MW, an increase of 22 percent on the previous year, but still far short of the 34,000MW needed to meet demand.

> "People are happy with solar power. The units really improve their quality of life. With fewer generators around, the air is cleaner, the electricity bill is smaller, and people are able to withstand the summer."

Mustafa Almola
Founder of Megawatt

Renewables offer some hope for alleviating pressure on the sector and reducing the heavy reliance on fossil fuels. Iraq has high levels of solar irradiance, making it ideally suited to solar power, but support for the fledgling industry has been limited. While regional leaders in the field, like the UAE and Jordan, have introduced subsidies and other incentives for renewables, Iraqi entrepreneurs face considerable hurdles.

"In other countries across the region, they have waived customs fees for bringing renewable energy materials, but in Iraq you have to pay bribes at the border, which drives the prices up," Almola says.

The road ahead

Using an Innovation Hub grant from Ideas Beyond Borders, Almola is buying equipment in bulk from abroad. "As a start-up, the biggest challenge is the cost of materials—I usually have to buy at premium prices from local suppliers," he says. The grant will enable him to order from a new factory in Jordan that produces high-quality renewable energy equipment, allowing him to offer more competitive prices for consumers, expand his business, and bolster the local market.

"There are only five renewable energy companies in Mosul, which is a very low number given the high demand," he adds, pointing to the dampening effects of under-investment and rampant corruption on the sector's growth.

There is some cause for optimism, however, as the government negotiates deals with foreign companies to construct solar power plants, including a recently announced $27 billion deal with French oil company TotalEnergies, which includes the development of an 1GW solar power plant in Basra—Iraq's hottest region—to supply the regional grid.

Many Iraqis feel that addressing the problems in the energy sector should be a government priority as extreme weather heightens the county's dependence on electricity. But the problems persist. In 2020, Iraq's then-prime minister Mustafa Al-Kahdimi said the country had spent at least $60 billion on the electricity sector since the 2003 US-led invasion that toppled Saddam Hussein, yet there is little evidence of progress resulting from this vast investment.

Almola's hope is that local projects can bypass the vested interests that govern national agreements and give people a chance to source their own solution to the power shortages they suffer every summer. "Mustafa is offering people in Mosul a viable response to an intractable problem," says Faisal Al Mutar, President of Ideas Beyond Borders. "Through him, we are investing in the evolution of a renewable energy market, supporting the shift away from fossil fuels and foreign dependence towards a sustainable local supply.

IDEAS BEYOND BORDERS   INNOVATION HUB

A pocket of peace in Baghdad

Rumi Café has become a favorite haunt for free thinkers in Baghdad

It's difficult to relax in Baghdad. Iraq's capital is tense and unpredictable, hardened by years of conflict that frequently spills into the streets. Residents are used to the sound of rockets and machine gun fire ringing through the night. They have seen the streets choked with protesters and felt the terror when security forces opened fire. Some even participate in the violence, working for armed groups or political parties that benefit from the turmoil. But most prefer to find respite where they can and forget for a while that they are forced to coexist with conflict.

Rumi Café in the Karrada area of Baghdad, is one of the few places people can do this, a rare sanctuary for authors, environmentalists, journalists, NGO workers, and others who dream of better days in Iraq as a whole. "We need somewhere to feel safe, so people can speak freely without any fear of oppression," says Mahdi Majeed, who opened Rumi Café in early 2023.

Mahdi Majeed with IBB's MENA project manager Rafal Al Adilee at Rumi Café in Baghdad

As a journalist, he saw the value in having a dedicated space for people to gather and exchange ideas. "I wanted to create the environment I needed, somewhere to debate thoughts, ideologies, and political movements," the 30-year-old says. But he also wants Rumi Café to be a place where people find respite from the pressures of life in this febrile city, so he named it after Rumi, the Sufi poet who is a symbol of peace and acceptance across the Arab world.

Majeed, who has won awards for his own poetry collections, wants the atmosphere to be calm and serene, channeling the compassion and creativity of the great Sufi master. To that end, he has filled the shelves with books to create a library, funded in part by an Innovation Hub grant from Ideas Beyond Borders. With the new library, Majeed hopes to reinforce the atmosphere of open discussion and debate, encouraging civil dialogue in a city where polarized views often end in violence.

"Baghdad is a difficult environment, and after a while, it gets to you," says Faisal Al Mutar, President of Ideas Beyond Borders. "Having a space to feel normal, be yourself, and engage with other people seeking the same respite is of huge importance—only people living in this city will fully understand why."

Already, there's a steady stream of regulars who come to work, socialize and relax at Rumi Cafe. Majeed has invested heavily in the food, compiling a selection of vegetarian, meat and fish dishes, including international and Iraqi favorites as well as a selection of pastries and the best-quality coffee they could find. "People love it," he says. "The food, the atmosphere, the space—most come every day."

■ IRAQ

Golden age glory

Medieval Baghdad was a place where scholarship flourished and ideas were welcomed. Artist Neshaat Al Shammari wants to revive this legacy through art

The Mustansiriyyah Madrasah by Iraqi artist Neshaat Al Shammari

At first, it's hard to recognize modern-day Baghdad in the paintings of Iraqi artist Neshaat Al Shammari. The grand structures swathed in light, with their palm-shaded courtyards and turreted facades, suggest a fabled realm where domed towers and ornate minarets rise serenely over a color-soaked city. But amid the blaring throng of Baghdad's busy streets, some of these sites still stand, rising out of the concrete as reminders of another era when a great empire emerged, and Baghdad became the center of the civilized world.

This period, from the eighth century until 1258, is known as the Islamic Golden Age, when the Arab world presided over the most progressive period of scholarship since ancient Greece, pioneering major advances in science, maths, astronomy, medicine, and many other fields. It was a time when Christian students learned Arabic so they could study in Islamic Cordoba and access the works of famous scholars, like ninth-century mathematician Muhammad ibn Musa al-Khwaririzmi, who laid the foundations for modern algebra, and Ibn Sina, (Avicenna) whose eleventh century *Canon of Medicine* was still required reading in Renaissance Italy centuries later.

The Abbasid caliphs who ushered in this era sought to unite the knowledge of the old civilizations and had texts in ancient Greek, Chinese, Sanskrit, Persian, and Syriac translated into Arabic, which became the international language of science for the next 700 years. Old ideas mingled with new translators, and scholars added their own thoughts, including the famed Arabic philosopher and mathematician Al-Kindi, who introduced the writings of Aristotle to the Arabic-speaking world, reshaping the debate around rationalism and religion.

It was a period of great scientific and cultural endeavor, yet there is little recognition of this illustrious heritage today. In a country riven by sectarian division, some even recoil from reminders of this era and dismiss the Abbasids as Sunni usurpers who enforced their illegitimate rule on the Islamic community. "They bring up their children to hate the memory of the Abbasids, and it's sad because this was our golden age," says Al Shammari, who lives between London and Baghdad.

His mission is simple—to celebrate the successes of the era and remind Iraqis of a cultural legacy that risks being erased by the conflict and destruction that has consumed the country in recent decades. Drawing on Iraq's rich heritage, he is using art to challenge international perceptions of his homeland by evoking the memory of the period when scholarship was seen as the summit of ambition.

"These people amassed a huge amount of knowledge; it's important to tell their stories," he says. Supported by an Innovation Hub grant from Ideas Beyond Borders, Al Shammari created the Baghdad Design Toolkit, a digital resource featuring designs based on the art and architecture of the era alongside accounts and anecdotes that tell its stories. "It's about bringing it alive and making it relevant for people," he explains.

A cosmopolitan capital

When the Abbasids overthrew the Umayyads in 790, they inherited one of the largest empires in the world. At its height in 850, their caliphate stretched from the North African coast to Afghanistan, covering the Middle East, parts of Asia Minor, and the tip of southern Europe.

To cement their authority, the Abbasid rulers built a new capital and invited the brightest minds to engage in the pursuit of knowledge and ideas that characterized the first few centuries of their rule. The early caliphs had learned from the failures of their Umayyad predecessors, whose discriminatory policies weakened their grip on power. Instead, they welcomed people of all faiths and cultures to their Madinat al-Salam, 'city of peace,' adopting a spirit of openness that fuelled the intellectual achievements of the golden era.

Scholars, philosophers, and astronomers flocked to Baghdad, drawn by the opportunities of this new academic age. Alongside them came merchants and tradesmen eager to participate in the commercial boom that transformed the Abbasid capital into one of the wealthiest cities of the day.

The city's prestige grew rapidly, particularly under the teenage prince Abu Ja'far al-Ma'mun, who made it his mission to own a copy of every work ever published. During his reign from 813 to 833, he sent emissaries abroad to source rare volumes from foreign libraries and often insisted that defeated rulers pay him in books rather than gold. The vast collection he amassed filled libraries around the new city, among them the famed House of Wisdom, where he launched his grand translation project to make the knowledge of the ancient world available in Arabic.

This is the inspiration and namesake behind Bayt Al Hikma 2.0, IBB's flagship translation project. "The golden age was a time when freedom of expression flourished in the Arab world," says Faisal Al Mutar, President of Ideas Beyond Borders. "By making works of science and culture available in Arabic, and supporting ideas through the Innovation Hub, we are drawing on the legacy of this era, when the pursuit of knowledge and enterprise was prized above all else."

Center of learning

Construction of the new capital began in 766 under the Abbasid Caliph Al-Mansur. Vast resources were poured into the project, with 100,000 workers and craftsmen hired to complete the city in just four years. Though nothing remains from this era, a handful of landmarks from the latter period of Abbasid rule still stand in Baghdad.

The Abbasid Palace and the Mustansiriyyah Madrasah, built by the Caliph al-Mustansir in 1233, have both been restored over the years, showcasing the intricate design that characterized Abbasid architecture. The Mosque of Umar Suhrawardi, which dates back to 1234, has also undergone several renovations, while the Wastani Gate, now an arms museum, is the only remaining example of four magnificent gates that once connected high walls protecting the medieval city from foreign incursions.

Unfortunately, there is little information at these sites to educate visitors about the age they represent. This has made Al Shammari's mission more challenging, particularly as much of Iraq's heritage has been removed from the country. "There is a legacy of looting when it comes to archaeology in Iraq," says Ashley Barlow, director of Creative Iraq, a UK-based consultancy that is supporting Al Shammari's project.

He helped Al Shammari mine through Arabic texts in the British Museum, British Library, the Victoria and Albert Museum, and other venues around the UK and US to find anecdotes and stories that bring this history to life. They also commissioned photographers to visit surviving sites in Baghdad and document the ornate arches, vaulted ceilings, and decorative stucco paneling that adorned Abbasid buildings. The result is a rich compendium of imagery and insights, tracing a path from the glories of the Golden Age to the legacy of this era in Iraq today.

Collapse of the caliphate

Art and architecture thrived under the Abbasids as the whirl of new ideas and creative endeavors infused the design studios of the day. Alongside the geometric and Arabesque forms commonly associated with Islamic art, Abbasid artists and architects drew inspiration from the human, animal, and plant kingdoms to enrich their work. Al Shammari has drawn on these traditions in a series of designs that will be freely available online and are intended for wide-ranging use, from jewelry making and clothing to ornaments and poster art. "Many things here are made in China, but we have this rich and huge history, so why not use it?" he says.

On the wall behind his desk hangs a painting of the Mustansiriyyah Madrasah. It is one of his, an oil on canvas of the university at dusk, with shafts of evening sunlight crossing the courtyards where Baghdad's brightest students once learned. It is a building that has witnessed much of the city's history, from its foundation as a global center of learning to the occupations, wars, and corruption that have torn at its soul countless times since.

Only a few decades after it opened, the madrasah witnessed one of the worst catastrophes to befall Baghdad in medieval times or in the centuries since.

IDEAS BEYOND BORDERS INNOVATION HUB

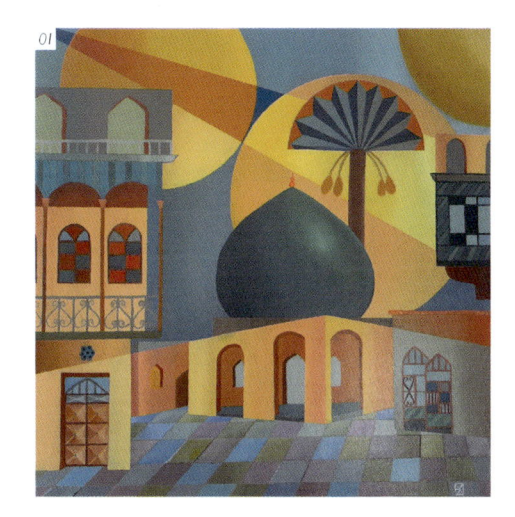

01. Sunlight on a Baghdad Square. Neshaat Al Shammari

02. Palms in the City. Neshaat Al Shammari

03. Artist Neshaat Al Shammari wants to inspire Iraqis with the achievements of the Islamic Golden Age

04. The Abbasid Palace in Baghdad. (Photo: Ali Namir Al-Nasseri)

📍 IRAQ

On February 13, 1258, Mongol forces entered the gates and laid waste to the city, slaughtering hundreds of thousands of citizens, including the caliph, in the siege of Baghdad. Many buildings were left in ruins, including the House of Wisdom.

This event marked the city's decline as a global center of culture and learning. That week in 1258, the Tigris River is said to have run black from the ink of books and manuscripts thrown into the water by the Mongols. According to the writings of an eyewitness, "So many books were thrown into the Tigris River that they formed a bridge that would support a man on horseback." Many ancient texts were lost for good.

No physical remains of Baghdad's central library have survived, but its legacy of connecting diverse peoples and empires through learning continues. Libraries and academic institutions bearing its name are found across the Middle East, linking modern education with this age of great learning, when knowledge was sought and celebrated above all else across the Arab world.

This is what Al Shammari captures in his painting of the Mustansiriyyah Madrasah, which he sees as "a symbol that knowledge and science transcends even the worst environments and that hope can be found in our surroundings."

IDEAS BEYOND BORDERS INNOVATION HUB

'Books gave me strength' – Sinjar's lone librarian

Yazidis have little access to books in Sinjar, but one man is carving out a space for culture in his war-ravaged heartland

Kamiran Khalaf, founder of Orshina

> "We have become a cultural monument in the city; any newcomers are immediately brought by locals to show that we do have culture here."
>
> **Kamiran Khalaf**
> Founder of Orshina

It was boredom that made life in Bersevi refugee camp unbearable, worse even than the squalid conditions. They were safe there, but that was all. Days dragged by, slow and relentless, with little distraction from the grim surroundings. No one knew what would come next. ISIS had rampaged through Sinjar, forcing the Yazidis to flee, and Kamiran Khalaf was among them— the lucky ones who escaped genocide only to end up here, in this no man's land behind coiled wire and high grey walls.

He was meant to be at university, studying to complete his degree; instead, he was stuck, unable to work or study or pursue any kind of dream. "Living in the camp was hell," says Khalaf, describing the grinding struggle to meet basic needs and the mental turmoil that made every moment arduous. The only consolation was books, so he read constantly, trying to escape the emptiness of life in exile. "For me, having books was a lifeline; even when I lost education, I could still gain culture and experience by reading," Khalaf says.

Access to books and education was extremely limited in the camp, so in 2015, Khalaf turned his tent into a library, allowing people to borrow his books for free. It was an immediate success. People flocked to his tent, particularly youth looking to reignite their studies or escape the drudgery of camp life. "Books gave me the strength to overcome stress and anxiety. They made me a better person," Khalaf says.

Over time, he amassed more than 600 volumes, building on his collection with donations from elsewhere. When he returned to Sinjar in 2017, Khalaf decided to establish a permanent lending library and book shop, hoping to reignite an interest in reading and restore a sliver of culture to his ransacked land. "This area was once well-educated; people used to be very interested in books, but since war erupted in 2013, that deteriorated. With the displacement of so many people, we lost access to the tools of education," he says.

Sinjar has been caught in multiple conflicts since ISIS invaded the region in 2014 and waged a murderous campaign against the local Yazidi population. When the militants were expelled in late 2015 they left a power vacuum that has since been filled by other armed factions, all fighting for control over this bitterly contested piece of land, which occupies a strategic position near the Syrian border in northern Iraq. Because of this, and insufficient funding from the federal government in Baghdad, reconstruction in the wake of war has been slow, with public services and basic amenities barely functioning. Around 70 percent of Sinjar's Yazidi-majority population remains displaced, with little incentive to return while their homeland remains in turmoil.

Khalaf was among the few Yazidis who did go back to Sinjar after ISIS was defeated in 2017. Almost immediately he set about finding a space for his books, renting land on the edge of a park in the center of the city. He opened the Orshina library in early 2018 and gradually added to a collection that now numbers 6,000 volumes, filling the shelves with novels, poetry, politics, and philosophy, as well as books on learning English and self-improvement, which are always a popular choice, he says.

But despite enthusiasm from his supporters, it hasn't been easy. "When I first had the idea, people actually opposed it and said it would be impossible, but now that they are starting to see the change I have achieved," Khalaf says. "We have become a cultural monument in the city; any newcomers are immediately brought by locals to show that we do have culture here."

Nevertheless, he faces constant harassment from political parties who see his library and its access to ideas as a threat to their agendas. "They don't want people being educated, they want to keep them on a leash, under their control," Khalaf says. In 2022, he was forced to close the library for six months due to political pressure but was eventually able to make his case in court and reopen. The harassment is ongoing—whenever he takes books to an event or applies for a job, he comes up against barriers from those who see books and learning as a threat.

"Yazidis are struggling to rebuild their lives in Sinjar, where multiple conflicts have stalled reconstruction and prevented many people from returning home. Orshina brings a ray of hope and a promise that progress is possible, even in the darkest of times," says Faisal Al Mutar, President of Ideas Beyond Borders. "Kamiran's desire to bring books to others is an inspiration. We need more people like him to help communities recover from the impact of conflict in Iraq and Kurdistan."

Khalaf has used an Innovation Hub grant from Ideas Beyond Borders to secure his financial situation and purchase a laptop to establish a record-keeping system and keep track of the books he loans out. Most days, he arrives at the library around 10 am and spends the day reading and writing his own novel, pausing whenever people come in to help them find the perfect book.

He stays until around 6pm and then locks up, hoping that the next day will pass smoothly without attempts to shut him down or prevent his work. At present, he is desperately searching for a lender to rent him space on private land so that he will be out of the government's reach. "I fear there might be at any time in the future, a government decision to make me abandon the land," says Khalaf. "That would be a huge loss to people in Sinjar."

IDEAS BEYOND BORDERS INNOVATION HUB

Books have been a lifeline for Kamiran Khalaf during difficult times

Orshina is a cultural sanctuary in war-torn Sinjar

◉ KURDISTAN

Kurdistan

New opportunities in Kurdistan

Walking through the bustling market in central Duhok, Hussein Ibrahim sees hundreds of faces from all over the world. His home has become a hub for people of diverse backgrounds and nationalities—Syrians seeking refuge in the Kurdish city, young people studying at its university, foreigners working in the development sector, and entrepreneurs forging new futures as opportunities open up across the Kurdistan Region of Iraq (KRI).

"There's a new sense of possibility here. I think in the next few years, we will see a vibrant entrepreneurial community emerge in Duhok and across Kurdistan," says Ibrahim, head of the Kurdistan office at Ideas Beyond Borders.

These days, he hardly recognizes the sleepy city he grew up in, where a trip to the market meant bumping into multiple people you knew. Back then, the only industries were farming or truck driving, and the working day finished at 3pm. "After that, you spent time with family or met friends in cafes to smoke shisha and drink coffee till midnight. Life was slower then, before everyone became so busy with work."

With the influx of people from all over the world, particularly in the aftermath of the war in Syria and the fight against ISIS, the character of the city has changed. "We see much greater diversity of people and businesses as new influences open up the private sector and create more opportunities in Kurdistan," Ibrahim, 43, says.

Barriers to business

The University of Duhok is one of the best in the KRI, and the campus buzzes with undergraduates from across the region. Many dream of starting their own business, launching social enterprises, and using their skills to solve problems across the

Leather goods by Kurd Wears. Kurdistan is becoming a hub for startups in the region. Image: Osama Al Maqdoni

Arab world. But like students across the regional border in Iraq, young people in the KRI struggle to find work, faced with soaring unemployment and a saturated job market that offers few opportunities to a growing youth population.

These problems are keenly felt in Duhok, which remains the poorest governorate in the Kurdistan Region of Iraq. An ongoing budget dispute between the central government in Iraq and the Kurdistan Regional Government has exacerbated the economic strain, leaving public sector salaries unpaid for months. Political divisions and broader security issues in the region further impede economic diversification as the government looks to develop the private sector and attract investor support.

These problems are mirrored across Kurdistan, where the lack of job opportunities translates into frustrated youth who are turning away from their homeland. "They see the opportunities in European countries or the United States and feel that this is the life they dream of. Instead of investing in their own country, they feel frustrated and left behind," Ibrahim says.

To him, the solution is clear. Working across multiple Ideas Beyond Borders programs in Kurdistan, including the Innovation Hub, he is striving to improve the environment for startups, bolster aspiring entrepreneurs, and champion projects that are denied access to funding. "We need to support our youth in developing their business plans. Too many good ideas that could benefit the country are going to waste," he says.

A regional hub for business

In recent years, the Kurdish Regional Government has pursued plans to reduce its reliance on public sector employment, strengthen the economy, and encourage private sector growth. Gradually, optimism is increasing amid significant strides in efforts to reduce bureaucratic hurdles for small business owners, pursue digital development, advance the banking system, and create a more attractive environment for investors and entrepreneurs.

As a result, Kurdistan is attracting talented youth from across the Middle East, bringing skills, solutions, and ideas to tackle its challenges and inspire change. "When you have a government that supports progress and works with NGOs to achieve it, people feel incentivized to pursue their ideas," Ibrahim says. "That is unique to Kurdistan; neighboring countries do not have this supportive environment."

At the grassroots level, a growing startup movement is empowering innovation through local support. In the southern city of Sulaymaniyah, Ranja Ali harnesses his extensive network of creative contacts to help talented freelancers find work. Many young people find it difficult to launch their careers in the city, so Ali decided to launch Wedonet, a freelancer network that operates with Innovation Hub support. "I really want Sulaymaniyah to grow. It could be a good place for freelancers and entrepreneurs, and I want to help make that happen," Ali says.

As the startup scene develops, more entrepreneurs are stepping forward with bold ideas. Ashraf Harba co-founded his B2B platform Meena six months ago to fill a void in the logistics space. An Innovation Hub grant enabled them to purchase a new laptop and printer, which will help manage the company's daily operations as it looks to expand. "There's a community of young people and small business owners who are coming together to confront the problems and make it easier for startups to operate," says Harba, 32, who moved to Erbil five years ago to escape the situation in Syria. "In the beginning, there was no infrastructure for business. Things are starting to change, but there are still problems for new enterprises."

A new environment for entrepreneurs

While the Kurdish government's ambitions mark a positive precedent in the region, significant hurdles remain. At present, influential members of government support the diversification of the economy away from its traditional reliance on oil. These elements are committed to private-sector progress, but others seek to protect their interests by facilitating corrupt networks and preserving the status quo.

"One of my biggest concerns is who will come to power in the next elections, but if our network stays in power, we can continue working with the Kurdish parliament to change the laws and support the startup sector," Ibrahim says.

Seizing the present opportunity, Ideas Beyond Borders launched a new project last year to improve the environment for small businesses and drive a new era of startup growth. The Kurdistan is Open for Business project aims to improve the infrastructure for entrepreneurs as they register startups while campaigning for pro-business legal reform in the region's parliament. This includes working with local NGOs and the Kurdish parliament to ease bureaucratic barriers for new businesses and amend outdated legislation that hinders aspiring entrepreneurs.

When Kamaran Safar registered his brand Kurd Wears in Duhok six years ago, the regulatory hurdles seemed insurmountable. "It's really off-putting. Eventually, the disadvantages outweigh the advantages, and you have to give up," he says. Safar, who secured an Innovation Hub grant last year, persevered to show other aspiring entrepreneurs that these hurdles can be overcome. "I have survived the setbacks because I want to make change through business and inspire other Kurdish youth to do the same," he says.

This is the spirit of camaraderie that the Innovation Hub hopes to foster as it empowers passionate individuals like Safar who pass on the benefits of IBB support. "Our aim is not only to empower the people we work with, but to share their success and show Kurdistan's young population that they too can create their own opportunities to succeed," Ibrahim adds.

Shared success

Already, progress has been made in digitizing company registration for new businesses and simplifying the bureaucratic process. Instead of traipsing between different government departments, entrepreneurs can now visit a one-stop registration website featuring advice on the legal requirements, investment prospects, brand development, and opportunities available through a growing network of incubators and accelerators across the country.

The Kurdistan is Open for Business project also provides grants and technical assistance to dozens of startups, with plans to launch a one-million-view social media campaign that will bolster Kurdistan's credentials as a destination for entrepreneurs. "When the Innovation Hub helps one person, they go on to provide economic opportunities for five more. That's the effect we are aiming to achieve," Ibrahim says.

Looking ahead, he is optimistic about the future of Duhok and Kurdistan. Recent decades have brought many changes to his city, but some things remain the same. "In Kurdistan, you can always rely on the support of your community; that's why people here are so resilient," he says. This is the spirit he wants to carry forward by helping a new generation of entrepreneurial youth pursue their ideas and empower one another.

"If we all do our small part, then we can create a huge network of young people who believe in themselves and believe they can build a life here instead of leaving," he says. "I think that is the hope young people need and want rather than taking the risky route to Europe and elsewhere."

Empowering entrepreneurs: A new era for business in Kurdistan

Ideas Beyond Borders has a plan to power startup success in Iraqi Kurdistan as the region seeks to become a hub for new business in the Middle East

Four years after opening the first leather workshop in the Kurdistan Region of Iraq, Kamaran Safar is used to seeing his designs on the streets of Duhok. The hand-stitched pieces have become popular among fashionable youth in the Kurdish city, and his small team is busy making bespoke bags, custom wallets, and laptop cases as word spreads and the interest in leatherware grows across Kurdistan.

"The market for these products is huge—there's so much untapped potential," says Safar. Starting from scratch meant that everything had to be imported from abroad. A simple leather wallet requires a blade, needle, thread, burnishing tools, bevelling tools, and paint. "You can't buy anything in person here," he adds.

Sourcing materials is one of the many challenges Safar has faced since launching his brand Kurdwears in 2018. While the business is doing well, the struggles of owning a startup have, at times, made him reconsider his decision to run a business alongside his career as a petroleum engineer. Much of this is due to the challenging regulatory environment in Kurdistan and a lack of support for new startups in the business sphere.

Safar has persevered, not to turn a profit, but to encourage other aspiring entrepreneurs by showing them that these hurdles can be overcome. "We can

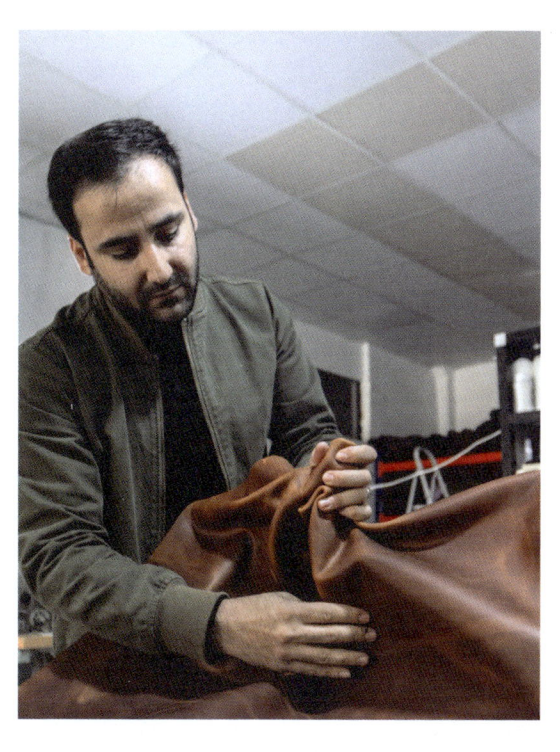

Kamaran Safar, owner of Kurd Wears.

KURDISTAN

do business for profit but why not use it for social change too? That way, if the business grows, so does the impact."

Fresh ideas

Recent years have seen a surge of startup activity in Kurdistan as the region cultivates its emerging status as a hub for startups and entrepreneurs. A population influx during the war in Syria and the battle against ISIS introduced diverse cultures, bringing fresh ideas and business opportunities to Kurdish cities like Duhok, Sulaymaniyah, and the capital Erbil. "Millions fled to Erbil during this time. It made the city more open to prosperous development," says Dr. Karzan Mohammed, founder of the Kurdistan-based Education and Community Health Organization (ECHO).

The interaction of different cultures created diverse opportunities across multiple sectors that transformed the business landscape and inspired a generation of young entrepreneurs. "People with new ways of doing business came to Erbil and started to open restaurants, cafes, and other enterprises. There was a transition as people in Erbil saw how to do things in different ways," adds Dr. Mohammed, who is working with Ideas Beyond Borders to modernize the environment for entrepreneurs and address the impediments that hinder startup success in Kurdistan.

High costs, cumbersome regulations, and difficulty accessing funding contribute to an inhospitable environment for new business at a time when Kurdistan, like the rest of Iraq, needs to diversify its economy away from oil and foster private sector growth. "The Kurdistan government wants to make the Kurdish capital Erbil a second Dubai," says Dr. Mohammed. "Now we're at a turning point. If things continue as they are for another five years, Kurdistan may lose its leadership in the startup sector."

At present, around 1.3 million people are employed by the government in Iraqi Kurdistan, which is struggling to fund a vast public sector payroll that accounts for 42 percent of its spending. With

Kurd Wears has created a market for locally made leather goods in Kurdistan. Images: Osama Al Maqdoni

high unemployment and a growing, mostly young population, empowering entrepreneurship and fostering startup growth presents a promising path towards prosperity, not just for Kurdistan but Iraq as a whole.

Making it official

Legal change is difficult under the current Company Law, which dates back to 1997, but momentum is building behind a growing appetite to modernize the landscape and open up opportunities on Kurdistan's business scene. The government's recently redesigned website outlines plans to "create the right regulatory framework to encourage foreign and domestic entrepreneurs, make it easier to do business in Kurdistan, and invest in infrastructure across the region."

Much of the focus is on supporting existing businesses through initiatives like Project Bloom, which provides loans of up to IQD150 million to established SMEs. Startups, meanwhile, face ongoing challenges to launch and survive the first few years as a new business. Kamaran Safar dreads the annual re-registration process when he is forced to take time out of his day job to traipse between the lawyer's office, his accountant, and multiple government departments to fill in the paperwork. For small startups like Kurd Wears, the lugubrious process can seem insurmountable. "To register Kurd Wears, I had to go through so many things. It's very difficult to start a business here," he says.

To avoid the bureaucratic maze, many small business owners operate unofficially, selling their products online and through informal channels. But without legal recognition, companies cannot engage with the mainstream market, shutting them out of opportunities to expand and undermining the dynamism of the sector as it looks to grow. "It's a real disadvantage because it means they cannot work with any official entities," explains Jomaa Mahmood Alikhan, programs coordinator at Rwanga Foundation for Development, which wants to create a culture of registering new business in Kurdistan.

Part of the problem is a lack of awareness around business regulations. With no clear source of information, young entrepreneurs are left in the dark. "They don't know the importance of being registered, so they don't bother—many just don't realize that unless you have that stamp, formal entities can't deal with you," says Alikhan, whose organization has partnered with Ideas Beyond Borders to create a pro-business climate and transform the landscape for new startups in Kurdistan.

IBB's Open for Business in Kurdistan project aims to create a one-stop registration website with all the information entrepreneurs need in one place, from videos on how to navigate the legal landscape to advice on securing investment, working with accelerators and incubators, building a brand and securing the proper support. It will also provide grants and technical assistance to dozens of new business owners and launch a one-million-view social media campaign to bolster Kurdistan's credentials as a destination for new business.

"Kurdistan has the potential to join Dubai and Saudi Arabia at the center of the free enterprise movement in the Middle East," says Faisal Al Mutar, President of Ideas Beyond Borders. "We are working with the Kurdistan parliament to achieve pro-business legal reform that will encourage investment and propel Kurdish business into an exciting new phase."

Looking ahead

Progress has already been made in simplifying the registration process for new businesses. On the government website, a new portal for online business registration is prominently displayed. It still takes up to a month, but the move to digitize the process is a welcome step for a generation of young entrepreneurs accustomed to operating online. It's part of a broader digitalization drive that will make it easier to cut through red tape and manage transactions online.

In Iraq's capital, Baghdad, efforts to move towards digital banking are already underway, but Kurdistan remains a cash culture, hindering the ability of startups to engage with international markets. "Lack of digital transactions is still a very big issue. People can't get money from their clients," Alikhan says. "If you have a skilled entrepreneur that is able to penetrate foreign markets, but cannot perform transactions online, then they cannot grow," he explains.

Ashraf Harba co-founded his B2B platform Meena six months ago to fill a void in the logistics space. All of their transactions are conducted in cash, but he hopes to move to online payments in the future. One of the main challenges they face with their startup, which connects retailers with wholesalers through mobile applications to facilitate the delivery of everyday food and household items, is currency fluctuation, which causes daily shifts in the price of goods. A grant from Ideas Beyond Borders enabled them to purchase a new laptop and printer, which will help to manage the daily operations of the company as it looks to expand.

"There's a community of young people and small business owners who are coming together to confront the problems and make it easier for startups to operate," says Harba, 32, who moved to Erbil five years ago to escape the situation in Syria. "In the beginning, there was no infrastructure for business. Things are starting to change, but there are still problems for new enterprises," he says.

At present, he is in Dubai, scoping out job opportunities and the possibility of one day expanding Meena to the startup capital of the region. However, the landscape is crowded and competitive in the Emirati city. His focus for now is on making it work in Kurdistan, where the support of organizations like Ideas Beyond Borders and efforts to improve the landscape for small businesses motivates him to keep going. "This program is changing things on the ground. It's going to be better for entrepreneurs in the future, I'm sure of it," he says.

Spending time in the Lotus Flower library has helped Surian process the trauma she endured under ISIS. Image: Osama Al Maqdoni

Women and girls rebuilding their lives after ISIS

Many women and girls in Kurdistan's refugee camps have been through horrific ordeals at the hands of ISIS. The Lotus Flower is helping them find a way forward

For a long time after fleeing the ISIS attacks in 2014, Surian was consumed by rage. She was a teenager when ISIS began its brutal genocide in Sinjar, killing around 5,000 Yazidis and forcing thousands of women and girls into sexual slavery. Now aged 20, she is stuck in a refugee camp, living in a crowded tent with few opportunities and an uncertain future ahead.

"I had anger issues and always felt down. I knew I needed to see a psychologist," she says. Surian wanted to rebuild her life, so she decided to sign up for training courses at a women's center run by The Lotus Flower, an NGO that supports women and girls affected by conflict and displacement in Iraq.

It was a positive step. "With the group therapy sessions and gender-based violence awareness, I am feeling calmer now—especially when I practice activities from the sessions," she says. The organization operates in three refugee camps across

📍 KURDISTAN

The Lotus Flower library is a space for Yazidi women to invest in their future. Image: Osama Al Maqdoni

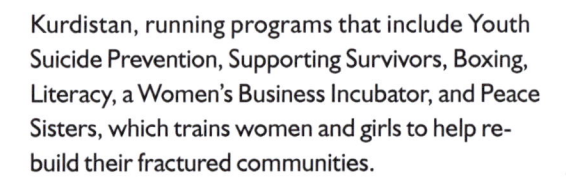

The popularity of their adult literacy classes prompted The Lotus Flower to establish a library. Image: Osama Al Maqdoni

Kurdistan, running programs that include Youth Suicide Prevention, Supporting Survivors, Boxing, Literacy, a Women's Business Incubator, and Peace Sisters, which trains women and girls to help rebuild their fractured communities.

Despite the impact of the pandemic, which saw many organizations withdraw or reduce their services in Iraq's refugee camps, The Lotus Flower has continued to grow, responding to mounting demand with new initiatives that aim to have a lasting impact. "We focus on the sustainable rebuilding of lives," says regional director Vian Ahmed. "We need more organizations like The Lotus Flower who are there for the long term and aren't going to leave after the emergency response."

The height of the Covid crisis was particularly bleak in Iraq's refugee camps. Cramped, unhygienic conditions made social distancing impossible, while the shutdown of services denied people their few sources of hope in a desperate situation. "Covid worsened the problems we're dealing with. We've seen a big spike in gender-based violence since the pandemic began, and we're facing much bigger mental health issues now," Ahmed says.

The Lotus Flower absorbed many of those left behind when aid agencies began pulling out, but with emergency funding shifting to Afghanistan and then Ukraine, resources are stretched. The biggest challenge, Ahmed explains, is core funding. Obtaining support for projects tends to be straightforward, but unrestricted core funding is vital, especially as we are growing fast and need to bring in new team members to support that."

But there are advantages to the organization's small team, which is faster and more agile than larger organizations weighed down by bureaucracy. "The key is that we have a passionate team, keen to make a difference," Ahmed says, pointing to the organization's founder, Taban Shoresh, whose own story of survival drove her to give up a career in London and dedicate her life to helping other women and girls rebuild lives decimated by conflict.

Shoresh was just four when her family narrowly escaped being thrown into a mass grave and buried alive during Saddam Hussein's Kurdish genocide. She remembers adults screaming and crying as they were taken to the site. At the last minute, they were rescued, but the family's trauma wasn't over. They spent months on the run during the Iran-Iraq

> "We need more organizations like The Lotus Flower who are there for the long-term and aren't going to leave after the emergency response."

Vian Ahmed
Regional director of
The Lotus Flower

Surian reading at her home in the camp.
Image: Osama Al Maqdoni

war, dodging bullets as the fighting raged around them. When they eventually made it to the UK, Shoresh faced other challenges, including ill health and an abusive marriage, but she has found ways to endure and now helps other women do the same through The Lotus Flower.

"It's about enabling women to build their own futures. We don't do it for them, instead, we give them the tools they need to make a long-term difference to their lives," Shoresh says. This includes developing skills to start businesses, particularly as many of the women they work with are widows or have lost their families and have no other means of support. Many have been through horrific ordeals at the hands of ISIS and have family members who are dead or still missing.

Others were just children when ISIS surrounded Sinjar in 2014 and began its extermination campaign. "All they have known is life in refugee camps and conflict," Ahmed says. As a result, they have missed out on their education, so The Lotus Flower runs adult literacy and English classes, which are often heavily over-subscribed. With more now able to read, the organization has established a library at its women's center in Essyan Camp with support from Ideas Beyond Borders.

"I saw the humanitarian crisis with my own eyes when I have visited the camp that The Lotus Flower works in. Building that library and empowering the Yazidis and other people there with knowledge and 21st-century skills hopefully will enhance their social mobility and help them in the short and the long term," says Faisal Al Mutar, President of Ideas Beyond Borders.

The space provides a place for women to learn, meet and work together, away from the grim monotony of camp life. "The library will be a lovely addition to the center," says Ahmed, adding that they also offer yoga and exercise classes there. "We want women to be able to enjoy the space, meet their friends, have tea and cake, then go into the library and pick a book to enjoy some quiet reading time."

The Lotus Flower library is simple, with no luxuries or modern conveniences, but it's safe, and there's a sense that life is moving forward there. For women and girls caught in the refugee cycle, it's a chance to gain knowledge, learn new skills, and build a different future for themselves.

KURDISTAN

Wedonet is revolutionizing work for Kurdistan's freelancers

A script writer, photographer, producer, and entrepreneur—Ranja Ali wears a lot of hats, and now he's using his experience to help others achieve their ambitions

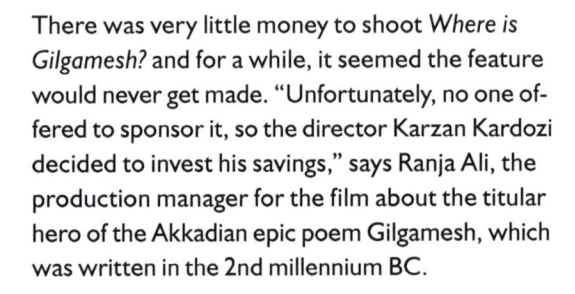

*Ranja Ali, founder of Wedonet
Image: Osama Al Maqdoni*

There was very little money to shoot *Where is Gilgamesh?* and for a while, it seemed the feature would never get made. "Unfortunately, no one offered to sponsor it, so the director Karzan Kardozi decided to invest his savings," says Ranja Ali, the production manager for the film about the titular hero of the Akkadian epic poem Gilgamesh, which was written in the 2nd millennium BC.

Making a feature film of this scale on a shoestring budget hasn't been easy. The team cuts costs at every opportunity, hiring rather than purchasing equipment, using accessible locations, and even getting family members to cook lunch. "We are breaking the rule of needing a lot of money to make a movie. This production will inspire other young people in Kurdistan to make films without needing lots of investment," says Ali, who is also a photographer and award-winning scriptwriter.

To bypass budget restrictions, he harnessed his extensive network of contacts to drive the project forward. When he's not filming, this is what Ali does best: bringing people together and providing them with the support they need to collaborate—a service he is now formalizing through his freelance network Wedonet.

Though just 23, he has already accumulated five years of experience with contacts across the film industry, arts, media, business, politics, and the development sector. Having dropped out of school at 17, he knows the challenges young people face to carve out a career in Kurdistan, and he's determined to make it easier for others to achieve their goals. "The mindset here sets people up to fail, but if they have good advice and strong support, they can do it," he says.

A graduate of Five One Labs, a well-known startup incubator in his hometown, Sulaymaniyah, in East Kurdistan, Ali has also traveled abroad and experienced the benefits of working in different environments. It's one of the opportunities he advocates when working with people at the beginning of their careers. "The problem is they don't travel, they stay in one circle, and you can't expand your vision that way."

Currently, he has around 65 freelancers in his network and clients ranging from international

IDEAS BEYOND BORDERS   INNOVATION HUB

media outlets and NGOs, to private businesses and politicians. "I might get a call from a journalist asking for a contact, or maybe someone needs a German translator for tomorrow or a photographer for a last-minute event… I put the request into Wedonet and make the best match."

The company takes a small commission for this service, but Ali is keen to expand the offering and create more opportunities for young people in Sulaymaniyah. "Wedonet is growing really fast, and we want to help as many people as possible," says Ali, who plans to provide workshops and mentorships through Wedonet to help more freelancers boost their careers.

Ideas Beyond Borders has awarded Wedonet an Innovation Hub grant to fund workshops and buy several laptops for the business. "Ranja represents the exact kind of person the Innovation Hub was created for. He knows that you don't need a degree, investors, or an established network. As long as you have the vision and drive, nothing is holding you back," says Faisal Al Mutar, President of Ideas Beyond Borders.

In the future, Ali wants Wedonet to be more international, with clients from all over the world investing in Kurdish and Iraqi talent. For now, his focus is on Sulaymaniyah and helping young people succeed while putting his city on the map for employers investing in the region's youth. "I really want Suli to grow. It could be a good place for freelancers and entrepreneurs, and I want to help make that happen," he says.

Just three hours from Kurdistan's business capital, Erbil, and with an emerging startup scene complemented by a comparatively liberal lifestyle, Sulaymaniyah has the potential to be a hub for Kurdish talent. "There's a kind of freedom here that you don't see elsewhere. It's a good place for young people—you can be you," Ali adds.

Ranja Ali on the set of a wildlife documentary being filmed in Kurdistan. Image: Osama Al Maqdoni

KURDISTAN

Making machines work

The Erbil Makers Hub offers a rare opportunity for aspiring engineers to hone their skills and develop prototypes for a new generation of machines

Mohammed Alsada at the Erbil Makers Hub, where he teaches design and engineering. Image: Osama Al Maqdoni

As a child, Mohammed Alsada used to break his toys on purpose. "I was really interested in electronics and manufacturing—I always wanted to know how they were made," he says. These days, he still spends his time coding, 3D designing, and tinkering with electronics, but now he has state-of-the-art machines and years of expertise to work with. His mission is to pass these skills to a new generation of makers in Kurdistan and enable people to convert their ideas into reality. "Everything is getting digitized and automated, so these skills are really important," Alsada, 32, says.

Across Iraq, automation and mechatronics engineers are in short supply, forcing private-sector employers to import labor from other countries. Part of the problem is the education system, says Alsada,

"They are makers with ideas to implement but lack the purchasing power for this kind of equipment, so it's a big deal to have it for them here."

Mohammed Alsada
Founder of the Erbil Maker's Hub

IDEAS BEYOND BORDERS　　　　　　　　　　　　　　　　　　　　INNOVATION HUB

Products range from artificial limbs and a motorized blind stick to an award-winning waste management machine and low-cost toys designed to keep children off smart-phones. Image: Osama Al Maqdoni

Students gather round a CNC milling machine, used to cut and engrave wood. Image: Osama Al Maqdoni

KURDISTAN

explaining that students often lack access to the proper training equipment. "These machines are expensive and hard to maintain, so students just learn about them without actually understanding how they work," he says. This is the gap he aims to fill through the Erbil Makers Hub initiative, which provides technical training and practical experience on a range of high-tech machines in its makerspace.

"Machines are always problematic and need people to maintain them. There is a huge need for such people here. Yes, we need entrepreneurship, but we also need a solution for this problem," Alsada says.

Inside the makerspace, students practice with different machines, getting a feel for the technology and its capacity to realize their ambitions. Laser cutters, a 3D scanner, CNC machines, fully equipped electronics benches, and multiple 3D printers work with different materials to create items ranging from affordable prosthetic limbs and waste reduction machines to home accessories, educational toys, and various product prototypes.

A new 3D printer, purchased with the proceeds of an Innovation Hub grant from Ideas Beyond Borders, is the latest addition to the space and will allow users to work with multiple materials at a much faster pace while filtering out the noxious gases often created during the 3D printing process. "Having access to this equipment unleashes their creativity," says Alsada, describing the students and entrepreneurs who frequent the space. "They are makers with ideas to implement but lack the purchasing power for this kind of equipment, so it's a big deal to have it for them here."

Alsada joined the space back in 2021 while working with an international NGO. When the NGO ended its operation in Iraq in 2022, he decided to keep the makerspace active and took on the cost and management himself. "I was determined to maintain the vibrant community we had built," he says.

It's time-consuming work. Most days, Alsada is there from 9 am until 9:30 pm, only leaving when the building closes at night. Alongside the workshops, there's the equipment to maintain, often with parts that can only be purchased from abroad. Costs climb quickly, but Alsada always finds a way to keep the doors open, building towards his future vision for the space. "I want this to be a big hub that connects creative minds—a place where anyone with an idea or special project can meet like-minded people, develop their skills, and support others in turn."

Key to this plan is keeping access to the makerspace affordable, so he runs digital manufacturing boot camps largely for free, meaning more people can benefit. Several of these initiatives, including the recent Product to Market Bootcamp program, were funded by the German Corporation for International Cooperation GmBH (GIZ), marking a positive step in ensuring the makerspace's continuity and growth.

Rawan Rashad, who recently graduated from the makerspace Product-to-Market BootCamp, which was implemented in collaboration with co-working space The Station, has created a motorized blind stick that alerts the user to potential obstacles. "The blind stick was actually fully designed, customized, and produced in the Makerspace and has features that I haven't seen anywhere else that could make a real difference to blind people," Alsada says.

Some makerspace projects have won awards, including Mohammed Hashim Ibrahim's waste management machine "Green Coupon," which sorts plastic bottles and aluminum cans and then issues coupons that offer discounts in supermarkets to incentivize recycling. Another startup creates low-cost toys for children to keep them off smartphones and provide them with more educational forms of learning.

Part of his work also includes helping to link employers with skilled graduates. Two of his former students have recently been promoted from engineers to supervisors, contributing to the growth of a specialized local labor force that benefits the private sector and creates opportunities for new graduates entering the market. "We have the people we need here; they just need to practice on the right equipment and build trust in themselves," says Alsada. "When they join, they are beginners, but by the end of the course, they have a new set of skills," he adds.

Sham concerts and ticket hoaxes: Fighting fraud in Sulaymaniyah

Psoola is transforming the ticketing industry in Kurdistan's cultural capital by investing in the region's burgeoning entertainment sector

January is event season in Sulaymaniyah, when the city gears up to host concerts, plays, and fashion shows in one of the busiest periods of the year. As the cultural capital of the Kurdistan region of Iraq, Sulaymaniyah has always been a hub for events, but it's only recently that residents have been able to book tickets without the fear of fraud.

"Ticket scams are rampant here. Con artists make up events, sell thousands of tickets, then run," says Shwan Sadiq, who founded the ticketing app Psoola to combat fraud. He remembers great excitement surrounding the news that Colombian singer Shakira would be performing in the Kurdish capital, Erbil. "There were adverts on television, posters in the mall and proper brochures. Tickets were going for hundreds of dollars," Sadiq, 29, says.

A day before the event, word spread that the concert had been canceled. A telephone line for refunds went unanswered. "The organizers were nowhere to be seen. The whole thing was a scam," he adds. That was a decade ago, but criminals are still using the same tricks to con people out of their money. In 2019, Sadiq and his family arrived at Spi Hall in Sulaymaniyah for a Hani and Frmesk Concert only to find that the gates were closed. "It happens all the time, even with charity events," says Sadiq.

Public advertisements on reputable platforms and high-profile names on the bill convince buyers to purchase tickets from unscrupulous vendors, but with no proper oversight, there is nothing to stop these elaborate schemes from happening again and again. Sadiq's concern is that they will undermine the city's entertainment sector just as it regains momentum following the COVID-19 pandemic. "We need to focus on reviving Sulaymaniyah's reputation as a hub for artists, actors, and musicians," he says.

His answer is Psoola, an application that sells event tickets online and protects buyers from fraud. The app, launched in 2021, has quickly become the default purchasing option for events across the calendar, facilitating ticket sales in live music, cinema, theater, motor racing, fashion shows, and conferences. "The concept was familiar because people have used similar platforms abroad, but no one had dared to invest in the ticketing industry here before," Sadiq says.

In the past, ticket buyers had to trawl vendors around the city to secure their preferred seats. With Psoola, a Wstreamlined interface takes users swiftly through the secure booking process online. People can also browse the app to view and book upcoming events, with a guarantee that their money will be fully refunded if the event turns out to be a hoax. "We don't transfer the money to the event manager until they start their event," Sadiq explains.

KURDISTAN

Psoola managed the ticket sales for the Ring Fighting League event in Sulaymaniyah, February 2024. Image: Osama Al Maqdoni

Shwan Sadiq, founder of Psoola

Online payments are not widely used in Kurdistan, where cash is still preferred, but Sadiq has found a way around this by collaborating with companies that sell top-up cards to make purchases online. "We are working on changing a culture, step by step," he says. "Our success will encourage others to enter the market and help us move the industry forward."

After securing an Innovation Hub grant from Ideas Beyond Borders, he now plans to launch a major marketing drive to widen his customer base before expanding to Erbil. Sadiq believes that home-grown businesses do better in Kurdistan, where people prefer to support local ventures over products and services imported from abroad. "This gives many people the courage to build startup businesses," he says.

The Kurdish capital, Erbil, has become a hub for startups in the region, with Sulaymaniyah close behind thanks to local incubators like Five One Labs, where a number of Innovation Hub grantees have cultivated business ideas and developed their skills as entrepreneurs. Recent changes to business registration procedures in Kurdistan have been welcomed as a step towards fostering the emergence of the startup sector and removing some of the barriers for new business owners, but significant challenges remain.

Last year, Ideas Beyond Borders launched the Kurdistan is Open for Business project, which aims to create a pro-business climate and transform the landscape for new startups in Kurdistan. Working with local NGOs and Kurdish authorities, the project will ease the registration process, provide grants and technical assistance to dozens of new business owners, and launch a one-million-view social media campaign to bolster Kurdistan's credentials as a destination for new business.

"Platforms like Psoola show what can be achieved when business is allowed to thrive," says Faisal Al Mutar, President of Ideas Beyond Borders. "This is the potential we are unleashing with the Innovation Hub and Open for Business in Kurdistan—supporting individuals who have found sustainable solutions to problems in their communities as they pursue transformative ideas with the potential to make a lasting impact."

IDEAS BEYOND BORDERS   INNOVATION HUB

Money, sex, revenge: The forces driving online violence in Kurdistan

Dr. Karzan Mohammed is uncovering a network of predators targeting women, girls, and young boys in Kurdistan

Dr. Karzan Mohammed knew there had been a rise in online violence against women in Kurdistan, but the results of his research still came as a shock. The abuse hadn't just increased; it had jumped six times in three years, confirming his fears of an online crime network targeting women and children in Kurdistan. The accounts were devastating. Young girls, some of them children, were being targeted by sexual predators online, tricked into handing over compromising photos, then blackmailed for money or sex, or sometimes as a form of punishment and revenge.

When they couldn't pay, their pictures were shared with groups on social media, circulated among hundreds or even thousands of followers, waiting for the next victim to go viral. "It has happened to so many girls, and we've seen several instances of suicide in recent years because of the shame and threat from their families," says Mohammed, the

Illustration by Lana Al-Jaf

KURDISTAN

> *"We wanted to send out a message to victims that the law is with them, parliament is with them—there are people working to address these issues."*
>
> **Dr. Karzan Mohammed**

founder of the Education and Community Health Organization (ECHO).

His team has spent the last two years gathering evidence to call for a change in the laws surrounding gender-based violence to include cybercrime and online harassment. In September 2021, they took their findings to the Kurdistan Parliament, where ministers agreed to revise the country's 2011 law on gender-based violence to incorporate measures against online crime. "We presented them with robust research so nobody can argue that this isn't going on," says Mohammed, who is calling for stronger legal protections and a dedicated cyber crimes police unit to prevent the problem from spiraling further out of control.

Mohammed, who is also the general director at Salahaddin University Research Center, is well-connected. His access to government department data and local authorities secures him the information needed to gauge the true extent of online violence against women and girls in Kurdistan. What he and his team have discovered is disturbing. Women, girls, and young boys are being systematically targeted by organized groups using blackmail to extort money or sexual favors via platforms including Snapchat, Facebook, WhatsApp, and Telegram.

"They approach the victims in different ways, and later, they use them to get to more victims. Once you are in their game, you have to bring in more people to get out," he says. In desperation, some victims feel forced to share photos of their friends to satiate their abuser. Others sink into despair and resort to self-harm, or live in fear of the consequences if their family finds out. As a 2022 report titled Online Violence Towards Women in Iraq states, "Sexual defamation has dangerous consequences, especially for women and girls who are at risk of "honor killings."

Until recently, the perpetrators of online violence were typically from other countries in the region, but the last five years have seen a marked rise in local groups targeting women in Kurdistan and Iraq. Mohammed points to a Kurdistan-based group called CTS, known for publishing pictures and videos of women in bulk. Led by an individual named Govand, the group exploits its victims in multiple ways, which include humiliating punishments, such as forcing them to come online and apologize to the group's leader in a live stream. According to a report in Rudaw, a number of victims were charged $5,000 to keep their photos private, but in some cases, they were published anyway.

According to Mohammed's findings, other local groups have copied this pattern of exploitation, with the rate of reported online abuse doubling every year. "Some groups do it for money and some for sexual gratification. Others use it as a form of punishment and power; they say you have disobeyed God, so now we will expose you to the whole community. And you don't know which one you will fall prey to," he says.

Usually, the women and girls targeted are unaware of the risks they face in the digital sphere. Perpetrators typically start a conversation on social media, often spending months gaining their confidence and cultivating a relationship online. When they eventually persuade their victim to share compromising photos or videos, the blackmail starts. "The community sees these women as guilty… online violence is a major cause of depression. You cannot speak out. You cannot tell your family or friends. It's a very lonely place," Mohammed adds.

Several people working with Govan's group have been arrested, but the ringleader remains at large and is believed to have gone abroad. Meanwhile, the group remains active with around 35,000 followers on their Telegram channel and a constant stream of pictures and videos exposing new victims to humiliation and despair.

In 2022, ECHO hosted the Cyber Harassment and Sexual Exploitation CHASE symposium funded by an Innovation Hub grant from Ideas Beyond Borders to tackle online crimes against women in Kurdistan. "We wanted to send out a message to victims that the law is with them, parliament is with them—there are people working to address these issues," Mohammed says.

Currently, the amendment, which adds online violence and other forms of abuse to the list of violations against women, has been delayed due to a dispute around sections designed to prevent marital rape and forced marital sex. At the symposium, ECHO announced a large-scale campaign with academics and institutions to educate the public and advocate for the amendment to pass in its entirety. In addition, Kurdistan's Ministry of Education agreed for the first time to include harassment and sexual exploitation in the national curriculum so that children aged 14 to 17 are aware of the risks and impact of these practices online.

"Sexual exploitation is a major issue, especially the direct targeting of Yazidis and widows who lost their husbands due to decades of war," says Faisal Al Mutar, President of Ideas Beyond Borders. "We hope our grant helps to empower a new generation to avoid exploitation by bad actors."

In the long term, Mohammed says, the emphasis needs to be on educating and empowering women and girls to ensure they are less vulnerable to these practices. "Most of the victims are poorly educated and are not free to leave the house," Mohammed says. He points to the high rate of unemployment among youth in the region. "They stay at home or sit in cafes smoking shisha and spend hours on their mobile. You need to empower, educate, and create opportunities for everyone. It's multi-faceted."

KURDISTAN

Spoken word in Kurdish

Our Stories is building a library of audiobooks in Kurdish, celebrating different dialects with a new body of literature online

There's a phrase used in parts of Kurdistan to describe people who went to school in Arabic-speaking communities. "They call them 'second-hand Kurds' because they don't speak 'proper' Kurdish" says Megan Kelly, pointing to a tendency for people to adjust their accents so they blend in.

Interpretations of Kurdish vary across greater Kurdistan, a region spanning four countries and cultures with multiple dialects spoken throughout. Two main languages predominate, with Kurmanji—the most widely spoken—common across Kurdish regions of Turkey and Syria, as well as parts of Iraq, while Sorani is used in Iran and across much of Iraq. Bahdini, a smaller dialect similar to Kurmanji, is spoken in Duhok, a governorate bordering Turkey and Syria.

For many Kurds, language is at the heart of a cherished Kurdish identity in a region where they have long been marginalized and forced to fight for their existence. But beneath this common cause, divisions between communities are reinforced by linguistic differences and the political affiliations they imply.

In the Kurdistan Region of Iraq (KRI), snap judgments can be made based on a person's dialect and accent. In the eastern city of Sulaymaniyah, people speak Sorani, which is often taken to mean they support the PUK, one of the major Iraqi Kurdish political parties. "If you speak Bahdini here, people might act like they don't understand you, even if they do, because to speak Bahdini is almost inherently aligned with the KDP," says Kelly, referring to the PUK's major political rival in the KRI.

"There is a curiosity to know what life was like under ISIS. Learning about it through books is a way to build understanding and empathy for displaced communities."

Megan Kelly
Co-founder of Our Stories

"That's the idea people have, whether it's real or not, which is a real barrier for people to have conversations," adds Kelly, who is hoping that a new literary project will help to break this down. Our Stories, launched with support from an Ideas Beyond Borders Innovation Hub grant, is producing a library of audiobooks from works published by authors across Kurdistan.

"The idea is not just to share local writing but to share local writing in local languages," says Kelly, pointing to the lack of audiobook material available in Kurdish dialects. The project emerged from a conversation with Ramazan Manaf, a volunteer-turned-colleague who suggested that audiobooks would help local authors share their stories with a wider audience.

By building an audiobook library, Kelly and Manaf hope to tap into the wider creative community, offering work to voice actors who struggle to find opportunities in Kurdistan. "There are very few roles for Kurdish speakers in film, so it's about figuring out how we can support this creative community and offer more opportunities to people," she says.

Our Stories is compiling a database of authors by contacting bookshops to find out which are their bestselling writers living in the Kurdish region. "They can write in English, Arabic, or Kurdish as long as they are based here," says Kelly, who hopes to include books in Kurmanji, Bahdini, and Sorani, as well as less-widely spoken local languages like Assyrian.

"A lot of the books available here are Western works that have been translated into Kurdish. We want to find out who's writing here and make their work available to local audiences," Kelly says. People in Kurdistan are interested in literature, but technology has changed how people consume media; making them available in audio format is a good way to reach a wider audience, she adds.

Historical fiction is a popular genre, and there's a particular demand for self-help books, which Kelly attributes partly to the social and political challenges that characterize everyday life in Kurdistan. In a region where advocacy is difficult, and the government frequently falls short in addressing the challenges people face, books help provide coping mechanisms. "If you're going to survive these structural issues, you do have to adopt this personalized approach to dealing with it," she says.

Books about life under ISIS are also in high demand. Cities in the KRI host a large number of displaced people from surrounding areas due to their relative stability. Duhok, which borders former ISIS-occupied Ninewa on one side, and Syria and Turkey on the other, has the highest number of refugees in the country and the second highest number of IDPs, despite its relatively small size, but all three major cities have seen significant shifts in the last decade.

"There is a curiosity to know what life was like under ISIS. Learning about it through books is a way to build understanding and empathy for displaced communities," says Kelly.

Many of those recently displaced are Kurmanji speakers now living in Duhok, where Bahdini is the dominant dialect. Kelly's hope is that the Our Stories audio library will widen access to Kurdish dialects for language learners who are hoping to adopt local tongues. "Audiobooks are a great way to learn behind closed doors," she adds, pointing to the dearth of learning materials available across all Kurdish languages.

By making more materials available, she hopes a greater understanding between Kurdish speakers will help to dissolve the divisions that exist, easing integration as people and communities adapt to demographic changes.

"For a really long time, life here was focused on survival. People have lived through sanctions, genocide, war, and economic collapse. We want people to have a chance to breathe and tell their stories, in the hope that this will legitimize creative interests and let people know these are worthwhile pursuits in this culture," she adds.

AFGHANISTAN

Afghanistan

Finding hope in Afghanistan

On 15 August 2021, Ahmad Mansoor Ramizy sat on a balcony overlooking the Afghan embassy in Ankara, Turkey. That was the day the Taliban stormed Kabul and seized power of the country he had lived in all his life. Tears flowed as he pictured his family home in Kabul and retraced the path along the river to school. How long would it be before he felt the familiarity of family gatherings on weekends, when 50 or 60 relatives would roast a sheep and feast together on hot summer days?

Growing up in Afghanistan was far from easy— bomb blasts, suicide attacks, and the chance of being mugged on the way to school were constant threats, but there was freedom and the sense of a future worth pursuing. Today, this Afghanistan feels like a distant memory and Ramizy knows it will be a long time before he can return home. Instead, he is helping his country from afar, bringing hope to communities that live under the Taliban.

As Afghanistan progam director at Ideas Beyond Borders, he finds and funds projects that educate and empower Afghan men, women, and children as they fight for a better future. To date, the Innovation Hub Afghanistan has distributed more than 50 grants to innovators across the country, creating new channels for knowledge and ideas to thrive. "With every new project we support, I feel energized that we have done a little bit of good for Afghanistan," Ramizy says.

Life under the Taliban

Almost three years of Taliban rule have transformed the country he knew. A day after the group seized power, the Kabul café, where Ramizy and his friends spent long afternoons discussing philosophy, science, and spirituality, closed alongside hundreds of other businesses representing a different Afghanistan. Media outlets were among the first to go as local

Illustration by Lana Al-Jaf

INNOVATION HUB

📍 AFGHANISTAN

Women in Kabul. Image: Paeez Jahanbin

radio stations, newspapers, and broadcasters folded, fled, or replaced their news coverage with Taliban-approved bulletins and recitations from the Koran.

At first, it seemed like a surreal nightmare. "The Taliban's takeover came as a shock for my generation; we had moved on from the idea of such a regime regaining power," Ramizy says. Now, the era he grew up in feels like a dream. "People back then were welcoming new trends, ideas, and initiatives. Those days were some of the sweetest memories that I proudly carry everywhere I go."

The new Taliban had no intention of adhering to promises made in peace talks, particularly when it came to respecting women's rights. Scenes of teenage girls sobbing as they were sent home from school beamed around the world, reiterating the Taliban's uncompromising position on women. Female university students soon followed as they banned Afghan women from education and most forms of employment, then many public places, including amusement parks, sports clubs, and even beauty salons. Most recently, a new edict to resume stoning women to death has been met with widespread horror.

For Ramizy's generation, growing up in the aftermath of the US invasion of Afghanistan, the shock of seeing their country collapse has taken its toll. Friends stuck in the country describe the depression that has descended, particularly among women who face a life behind closed doors. "They feel that this is the end of the world and it's dark days from now on. Their accounts of what's happening are harsh and horrible," he says.

> *"The Taliban's takeover came as a shock for my generation; we had moved on from the idea of such a regime regaining power. People back then were welcoming new trends, ideas, and initiatives. Those days were some of the sweetest memories that I proudly carry everywhere I go."*

Ahmad Mansoor Ramizy
Afghanistan program director at Ideas Beyond Borders

Lashings, disappearances, and atrocities — the nightmare stories of their parents' youth are being re-lived by a new generation of Afghans whose futures evaporated overnight. Yet Ramizy refuses to relinquish hope. In 2021, he joined Ideas Beyond Borders to set up the Voice of Science podcast and launch the Innovation Hub in Afghanistan, empowering young Afghans to pursue a better life.

"This is exactly the position our parents were in under the first Taliban regime. Then the US intervened and everything changed." This time, he says, the change must come from within. The Innovation Hub supports opportunities for people whose lives have been upended by the return of the Taliban regime. "We are trying to motivate people and give them hope to continue their education, continue seeking knowledge," Ramizy says.

Creating opportunities

The Innovation Hub's flagship project, Underground Schools in Afghanistan, has raised almost $100,000 to support girls who continue their education in secret. Students take different routes to class to evade notice and gather in a backroom with the blinds drawn. Despite the precautions, it's dangerous for these girls to continue learning, but many feel there's no other choice. "They want to be educated to create a country at peace. They believe the danger of staying quiet and illiterate is greater than the current danger, which is the result of illiteracy," says Salma*, who teaches them from a secret location in Kabul.

Education is a significant theme among Innovation Hub projects in Afghanistan, some of which focus on specific requirements, like English language or coding bootcamps to help Afghan women meet the criteria for scholarships abroad. Others prioritize skills for employment so Afghan men and women can set up workshops at home or secure online jobs with companies overseas.

Samiullah Nazari set up his company Inspirand to connect freelance web developers in Afghanistan with organizations in Canada and the US. As international funds were withdrawn and Afghanistan's economy collapsed, he wanted to help talented Afghans find work. "The situation in Afghanistan is terrible at the moment, but by building a bridge between these two markets, we can create the access and eligibility people need to get hired and eventually find a way out," says Nazari, who secured an Innovation Hub grant to continue his work.

In the future, Ramizy hopes to create a network of innovators like Nazari to collaborate on bold ideas, but in today's Afghanistan, it's safer to isolate contacts and evade the notice of the Taliban. For now, it's enough to provide people with the funding they need to withstand the onslaught against their freedoms. "A few thousand dollars goes a long way

* Ideas Beyond Borders uses pseudonyms to protect the identity of our partners in Afghanistan.

in Afghanistan. It's a once-in-a-lifetime opportunity for many of the folks we support," he says.

Prioritizing progress

The Innovation Hub prioritizes people who are unable to secure funding through other channels, bypassing the lengthy forms that can alienate aspiring applicants. "Some people aren't able to write detailed proposals and submit complicated budget reports," Ramizy says. "The Innovation Hub is like a training ground where they learn the skills to shape a project and build a track record before approaching bigger sources of funding."

Short applications also enable Ideas Beyond Borders staff to process proposals efficiently and get the funding across fast. When an education center attended by students from the minority Hazara population in Kabul was targeted by a suicide bomber in September 2022, it took just a few days for IBB to provide funds to rebuild the school. At least 53 people were killed in the blast, and more than 100 were injured, but within a matter of weeks, students were back at class, refusing to relinquish their right to learn.

"Countless times this has happened in this area, but people here still want to fight and continue the struggle for their right to education," Mukhtar Modabber, who founded Kaaj Education Institution, told us. He lost his sister in that attack but pushed grief and trauma aside to focus on restoring the school. "We cannot stop — if we do, these kids' futures will be destroyed, and we will have more violence and outrage in society," Modabber said. "This is our way of pushing back against injustice and fighting towards a better future," he added.

It's this philosophy that drives many of our innovators in Afghanistan as they struggle to uphold shared values at great personal risk. As the Taliban tightens its grip on the country, their voices are a last line of defense against the darkness that's descending. "The more people we line up with us, the stronger our front will be against darkness, violence, and dogmatism," Ramizy says.

Looking to the future

What worries him most are the changes taking place in Afghanistan's schools, where the curriculum has been re-written to reflect Taliban beliefs. "Children are getting this heavily censored version of Islam with a radical and racist ideology attached — a package of radical extremism is being spoon-fed to Afghan kids," he adds.

With half the youth population shut out of education and the other half receiving a Taliban-influenced curriculum, access to knowledge and ideas must remain. Most important, Ramizy says, is that people remember they have choices. Documenting his escape from Kabul in 2021, he writes: "People inside the country must be made aware of the sweet taste of liberty, freedom, and what it feels like to have a choice over your life and your way of thinking …"

"My country is now a slave to dogma and religious indoctrination that will haunt my generation and the generations to come. Yet I remain hopeful that through my work with Ideas Beyond Borders and Voice of Science, I will be able to take part in bringing about the Afghanistan that my countrymen deserve."

Afghan girls learning in secret.
Image: Madina Qati Musadiq

Living under oppression: Afghan girls continue classes in secret under Taliban rule

Afghan students are defying the ban on female education at an underground school in Kabul

The blinds are drawn in Layla's* classroom and the atmosphere is tense. A member of the Taliban could bang on the door at any moment. Even so, she loses herself in the lesson, forgetting for a while that this isn't an ordinary school and life as she knew it before Thursday, 12 of August, is unrecognizable. That was the last day she attended class as usual. Over the weekend, the Taliban swept into Kabul, and by Monday, her school was closed.

"I was thinking that the world and life is just finished. I cannot go to school, I cannot go to university in the future and be a great person, because they want women and girls to just sit at home and do nothing," the 17-year-old says.

When schools reopened across the country weeks later, only boys were allowed back. Later, primary school girls returned to class, but from

AFGHANISTAN

Ideas Beyond Borders supports several secret schools for girls in Afghanistan. Image: Madina Qati Musadiq

7th grade on, they remain barred. "I am tired of war and backwardness… if I cannot study, I will stay as weak as I am today," says Layla.

In January 2022, Taliban officials repeated promises to reinstate education for all girls but then extended the ban indefinitely. In the months that followed, a series of Taliban directives imposed further restrictions on women, barring them from most forms of employment, limiting their freedom of movement, and banning them from many public places. "Our mothers and sisters are illiterate because of their wars. I am afraid history is repeating itself in Afghanistan," says Salma*, who was a teacher at a private school in Kabul before the Taliban takeover.

Afghan women persist with underground education

At her students' request, Salma is running a secret school for women, teaching twice-daily mathematics classes at an undisclosed location in Kabul. "Even one day, one week, or one month more learning might help my students stay motivated," says Salma, who received an Innovation Hub grant and additional support from a special fund set up by Ideas Beyond Borders to support underground schools in Afghanistan.

In a handful of provinces, education institutions have struck deals with local Taliban officials to allow secondary school girls back to class, but for anyone else defying the ban is extremely dangerous. Women and girls have been arrested by the Taliban and in some cases disappeared after evading the group's restrictions, but Salma's pupils keep coming because they are more scared of a future defined by the Taliban. "They want to be educated to create a country at peace…. They believe the danger of staying quiet and illiterate is greater than the current danger, which is the result of illiteracy," she says.

She takes what measures she can to ensure their safety, holding classes in a secret location, changing lesson timings so they aren't seen leaving at a specific hour, and advising them to travel individually rather than in groups to class. "Actually it is beyond my ability to protect them… I am afraid of being punished, whether me, my team, my students, or my family."

If a Taliban official bangs on the door, she will sweep the books aside and tell them the women are doing Islam Studies and Quran training. Aside from a whiteboard, there is little else to indicate that this is a school. Students sit cross-legged on the floor in the corner of her house, with the doors and windows closed. "It's very different to a normal

> *"It's very different to a normal school day, but at least the purpose is the same, which is educating the girls at any cost, regardless of the challenges we face."*

Salma*
Teacher at a secret school
for girls in Afghanistan

school day, but at least the purpose is the same, which is educating the girls at any cost, regardless of the challenges we face," she says.

Afghanistan had seen a steady rise in female education since the former Taliban regime, which ruled the country from 1996 to 2001 and banned girls over the age of eight from school. In 2003, just six percent of Afghan girls were in secondary school, compared to 39 percent in 2017, according to World Bank figures. Female education was seen as a success story during the 20-year occupation of Afghanistan, but since the fundamentalist group regained power following the withdrawal of US troops from the country, that has been placed on hold.

In the months after the fall of the Kabul government, The United Nations called on the Taliban to avoid reversing two decades of progress in education, assuring Afghan women that their future remains a priority for the international community. "You can be assured that we will continue to amplify your voices and make it a zero condition that girls must have an education before the recognition of any government that comes in," Amina Jane Mohammed, Deputy Secretary-General of the United Nations said when teenage Afghan girls learned they would not be returning to school.

Since then, they have discovered what their aunts and mothers endured under the former Taliban regime—a dystopian nightmare brought brutally to life. "I had read books about what they did the last time they came to my country," says 19-year-old Nadia*, who was born after the US ousted the first Taliban regime.

She had planned to pursue higher education and a career in public service before her world narrowed overnight. Now, she attends Salma's underground school, which provides a glimmer of light in a life that has otherwise gone dark. "This is the only time I study and do something for my future," she says. 'I can just get away from the stress at home and thinking about my ambiguous future in Afghanistan."

* The names in this piece have been changed for security purposes.

AFGHANISTAN

Illustration by Lana Al-Jaf

Slipping past Taliban censors

Meet the female journalists risking all to tell the truth and fight for a better future in Afghanistan

Sana* used to love traveling for work in Afghanistan. As a journalist, she visited provinces across the country, covering events on the ground. When a new story came up, she would book a flight, throw her things in a bag, and head to the airport. "We would just send a last-minute message to our families to let them know where we were going. That's how safe and relaxed it was," she says.

These days, life looks very different for journalists in Afghanistan, particularly women who are barred from most forms of employment by the Taliban.

Traveling, even the short distance to Kabul from Sana's home in Bamiyan Province, is now extremely difficult. "Women who travel without a male companion are questioned a lot. The Taliban members turn away as though disgusted to talk with them. That's how these people react to women," she says.

When the Taliban seized power in August 2021, thousands of journalists fled Afghanistan. New regulations were announced, curbing press freedom and forcing many outlets to close. A decree issued by Taliban supreme leader Mullah Haibatullah Akhundzada in July 2022 warned that "defaming and criticizing government officials without proof" and "spreading false news and rumors" was forbidden. Those who "slander" government employees will be "punished," he said.

In the space of a year, Afghanistan lost 60 percent of its journalists as the Taliban reshaped the media landscape into a propaganda platform for the regime. These findings, published in a survey by Reporters Without Borders, show that female journalists were the hardest hit, with 76 percent losing their jobs.

The situation has since deteriorated further. The few remaining domestic media agencies are closely monitored, and many reporters self-censor to avoid antagonizing the regime. Just a handful of journalists inside the country report the truth, working in secret to keep the world informed. These journalists undertake significant risks to ensure the horrors happening at home are broadcast overseas as the Taliban attempts to erase reality and establish its legitimacy as Afghanistan's ruling regime.

The Taliban's edit

Speaking to the BBC in the aftermath of the takeover, a member of the Taliban's social media team discussed their strategy. "Most Afghans don't understand English, but the leaders of the Kabul regime actively communicated in English on Twitter—because their audience is not Afghans but the international community," he said." Social media is a powerful tool to change public perception… We want to change the perception of the Taliban."

The approach stands in stark contrast to the first Taliban regime in the nineties, which banned the internet and smashed up television sets. Today's Taliban is media savvy, harnessing social media to engage with Afghans and cultivate a fresh image online. One trend features YouTubers posting videos of themselves as they stroll around Kabul, eating in cafes and interacting with women and foreigners to show a supposedly safe and peaceful side to Afghanistan under Taliban rule.

"It's a viral trend in Afghanistan at the moment," says Ahmad Mansoor Ramizy, Afghanistan Program Director at Ideas Beyond Borders, pointing out that Taliban minders are often present in these videos. "These reporters propagate the Taliban agenda, which doesn't tell the true horror story of what is going on in the country," he says.

When the Taliban first seized power in 2021, there was some suggestion that they would stand by promises to respect human rights, including access to education for women and girls. That hope quickly dissolved as they barred teenage girls from school and rolled back the rights of women with strict limits on dress and conduct, compelling them to stay at home and limit their presence in public life.

Meanwhile, reports of torture, disappearances, public floggings, and executions revealed by local reporters and rights groups show how quickly Afghanistan has reverted to the darkest days of the first Taliban regime. A culture of fear prevents many from speaking out about family members who have been tortured or murdered, in case of retribution. "The Taliban will do whatever possible to cut people off from information and the outside world. This is where the work of the journalists supported by Ideas Beyond Borders can make a difference," Ramizy adds.

Culture of fear

Journalists like Sana and Tamana*, who continue to uncover the truth at great personal risk, know that at any time, they might be discovered. "The Taliban sees reporters as spies. If they find us reporting, especially for a foreign media agency, it would put our lives in danger," Tamana explains. "At the very least, they would stop our work and put us in prison." Reporting in the streets, she is careful to keep a low profile. "Even holding a phone makes us suspicious," she says.

Researching the circumstances of female drug users in Afghanistan for a recent story, she used a fake ID card and conducted the interviews in secret with help from a friend at a Taliban-approved media agency.

◉ AFGHANISTAN

Tamana works for an organization called Radio for Peace International, which received an Ideas Beyond Borders grant to produce a series on the stories of Afghan women. The program's coordinator, Jamila Karimi, was forced to flee Afghanistan shortly before the Taliban seized power. Now she is helping female reporters to continue their work on the ground because she sees it as one of Afghanistan's last hopes. "Saving gender journalism means saving a diverse society and ensuring pluralism in the country," she says.

For a while, before the Taliban regained power, life was improving for female reporters in Afghanistan. "We could report on location, go to offices freely; it was good. In rural areas, people had a more traditional mindset and were not comfortable seeing a woman with a camera, but for the most part, female journalists were normal," she says.

But as the Taliban expanded their influence across the country, that began to change. In 2020 and 2021, there was an alarming rise in threats and attacks against journalists as the insurgents grew brazen in their attempts to stamp out free speech. After a colleague was assassinated, Karimi and her husband went on the run, hiding at a hotel in Kabul, before moving to Uzbekistan.

"We felt the danger among the journalist community—there were calls and texts from the Taliban threatening us," says Karimi, who worked as a reporter for Pajhwok Afghan News, a leading news agency in Afghanistan. The platform, which still describes itself as 'Afghanistan's largest independent news agency' is among those that continue to operate in Afghanistan, but a disclaimer on the platform's website reminds readers of the pervasive presence of the Taliban's watchful eye:

"Given the current situation in Afghanistan, the reporting situation for Pajhwok staff is not always safe, so, to protect our teams, we may not always be able to report all sides of a story or may need to delay publication of some details, due to threats on our staff."

"The Taliban sees reporters as spies. If they find us reporting, especially for a foreign media agency, it would put our lives in danger."

Tamana*
Afghan journalist

Resisting a new reality

It's not just the security situation and Taliban censorship that are making life difficult for journalists in Afghanistan. The country's economy is close to collapse, starved of its lifeline from international aid programs.

For most Afghan reporters operating in secret, overseas funding from organizations like Ideas Beyond Borders is the only means of sustaining their work. Hoor Sabah* launched her online magazine Zane Rooz in November 2022 to tell the stories of Afghan women under the Taliban. "We are shedding light on the horrible atrocities the Taliban and their people are committing. Otherwise, people will become accustomed to what they are seeing and start to accept this new reality," the 26-year-old explains.

One incident she covered revealed the suffering of a woman who was beaten to death for defying her husband by visiting her mother without his permission. The Taliban released him without charge. "These cases are very difficult for us to comprehend, very shocking and disturbing. Nobody mainstream is talking about them because they can't," she says.

This culture of silence makes reporting these stories vital, not just to show the outside world, Sabah says, but to remind Afghans that these violations must never become normal. "While we can't save the people in these stories, we can help shape society and save women in the future."

An IBB grant covered the first six months of operation, enabling her to launch Zane Rooz and hire reporters to gather stories from across the country, including remote parts of Afghanistan. With fewer journalists on the ground, it is increasingly difficult to access women in rural communities, where fear prevents people from speaking out about violence and abuse.

Most of the journalists that remain are based in Kabul and, with travel restricted, it's difficult to shed light on cruelties perpetrated elsewhere. In its report, Reporters Without Borders found that, of the 2,756 women journalists and media workers employed in Afghanistan prior to August 2021, only 656 were still working a year later and, of these, 85 percent were in Kabul.

"Looking at the future Afghanistan faces, it's more important than ever to find ways of amplifying the few voices still finding a platform for the truth," says Faisal Al Mutar, President of Ideas Beyond Borders. "Without these brave individuals, our view of Afghanistan would be restricted, and the Taliban's violent campaign against women would be hidden from the world."

Sabah's male colleagues work in an office, but she and other female members of the team work from home, aware that any day they might be discovered by Taliban officials, who conduct house-to-house searches and question people in the street. But, while the fear of discovery hangs over her as she works, Sabah refuses to stay silent. "If we don't take this risk, nobody will know what's going on," she says.

Untold suffering

For Sana too, the toll of telling these stories is a heavy one. Sitting with women as they unburden their struggles in hushed tones, she listens and consoles, offering what little comfort she can because these days, there's nothing else. "If a woman is abused and has troubles at home, nobody is going to listen to her; no court will prosecute her case. The least I can do is listen, let them express their thoughts, and talk about what they went through," she says.

Many have nowhere else to turn. One woman Sana spoke with was hospitalized by her husband for querying his decision to take a third wife. His family had a relationship with the Taliban, so she stayed silent, afraid they would take revenge on her father or brothers if she uttered a word. "It brings me to a state of shock knowing that in the 21st century, this still happens," Sana says. "There is a sense of hopelessness to see people in other countries live with rights, liberty, and freedom when in Afghanistan, women are prosecuted just for being female. It's painful that I can't do anything about it other than listen."

Returning home in the evenings, she feels altered by the suffering she has seen. "I get upset, unsettled, even my relationship with my family is different when I hear these things." But she perseveres, hoping that one day she will make a difference in bringing these stories to light. "When I leave, I tell them everything will be okay. They are empty promises, but at least it brings comfort to them," she says. "And they are happy knowing that somewhere around the world there are people and organizations that are interested in hearing what they have to say and understanding what they are going through."

The names in this piece have been changed for security purposes.

📍 AFGHANISTAN

Picture this Afghanistan: Historic prints recall better days

A digitization project reveals Afghanistan's heyday when education was equal, women were freer, and the country was on the cusp of progress

Thousands of historic photographs showing Afghanistan between 1940 and the 1990s will be available online. Image: Paeez Jahanbin

Women mingle with men at a political demonstration in Kabul, 1970. Image: Nancy Dupree Collection, Afghanistan Centre in Kabul University (ACKU)

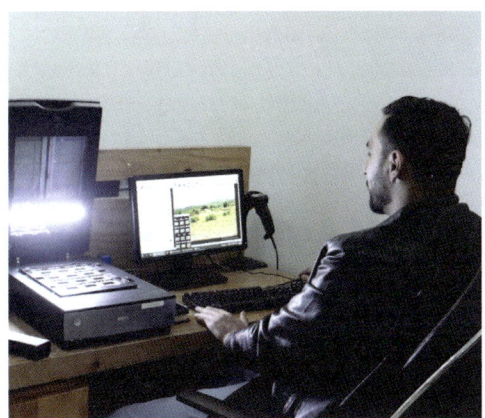

The images show a different side to Afghanistan. Images: Paeez Jahanbin

Few Afghans would recognize their country in Osman Hamdard's photographs. They show women at a political demonstration in Kabul, chatting freely with men in a public square. In the foreground, one woman holds up a placard while others mill around behind her, several dressed in skirts. In 1970, when the picture was taken, this scene was normal, but today, these women would risk punishment for failing to observe strict dress codes and appearing in public without a male escort.

"This is something the current generation has no idea of. They have never seen it," says Hamdard, who is digitizing thousands of historic photographs to preserve this vanishing past for generations to come. Another image from 1976 is even more at odds with contemporary Afghanistan. In the faded, sepia-hued print, two women handle heavy machinery at a Kabul factory, one driving a truck, the other moving a large piece of equipment into place. "It's eerie and depressing to see that 50 years ago we had this, and now we are a hundred years back," Hamdard adds.

The images he is digitizing, which show Afghanistan between 1940 and the 1990s, are part of a vast collection left to the Afghanistan Centre in Kabul University (ACKU) by Nancy Dupree, an American archivist who championed the country's culture and heritage for more than half a century. "It was one of the wishes outlined in her will to digitize the images and make them available to everyone," says Hamdard, quality control officer at ACKU, which holds around 12,000 images left by Nancy and her late husband, Louis Dupree.

Many of the pictures capture the country during its 1960s heyday when Nancy first traveled to Afghanistan as a young woman. Some date back even further—to the early 1900s and the period when Afghanistan gained its independence in 1919. These show a country in transition as Afghanistan went from royal rule to republic before undergoing a massive modernization drive during the 1960s when, for a brief period, it was known as "the Paris of Central Asia." This was a golden era, when the streets were clean, and new houses were being built as foreign investment flooded in, funding development programs across the country.

AFGHANISTAN

A woman having a fitting in 1960s Afghanistan, when dress codes were more liberal. Image: Nancy Dupree Collection, Afghanistan Centre in Kabul University (ACKU)

Standards of living rose rapidly as unemployment fell and education became available to all, with women studying alongside men at school and university. Afghanistan was still a poor country, but it was making progress, and the mood was optimistic as tourists came from all over the world to admire the beautiful gardens, historic architecture, and snow-capped mountains towering over Kabul. "The pictures of this era depict a very different Afghanistan to the one we know today… by preserving them, we are showcasing this different vision of Afghanistan to the next and future generations," says Hamdard.

An Innovation Hub grant from Ideas Beyond Borders will enable ACKU to digitize 1,000 prints from Dupree's collection. Hamdard worries about preserving the rare slides in Afghanistan's humid environment and is keen to progress as rapidly as possible with the digitization project.

"We must never forget that not all progress is positive. The last 50 years in Afghanistan have seen a society regress into terror, authoritarianism, and blind theocracy. Osman Hamdard's work is dangerous to the current regime for this very reason: it is a testament to a time when Afghans were free. The Taliban know that these memories will eventually be the foundation for Afghanistan's brighter future." says Faisal Al Mutar, President of Ideas Beyond Borders.

It's labor-intensive work and requires thorough research. Luckily, Nancy Dupree was a meticulous record keeper, numbering the prints in turn and then jotting down descriptions in her notebook, chronicling each image's time, place, and subject matter. Catalogs donated by other sources, which number around 7,000 prints, can be harder to pin down. ACKU has to piece together the story behind each image so they can pass it on to current and future generations. "Some of the pictures are easy and come with notes on the back, but others have no information at all, and it takes a lot of time," Hamdard says.

Up to 200 people visit ACKU each day to access the papers, books, photographs, and other resources stored in its archives, while over 7,000 users login to access its historical photograph collections online. In total, ACKU houses more than 190,000 documents, and Hamdard is determined to put as much as possible online for students, researchers, and other interested parties to access worldwide. "History is a pathway to the future, and we want to publish the rich history of Afghanistan and make it available to everyone," he says.

The photographs are an essential part of this project. Alongside the images of everyday life are snapshots of historic sites, including the famous Buddhas of Bamiyan, which the Taliban destroyed in 2001. There are black-and-white pictures of royal rulers, including Khairya, the daughter of Mahmud Tarzi, who set the trend in wedding dresses with her European-style bridal gown worn at her wedding in 1909. A later picture in color shows a seamstress fitting a female customer in the 1960s, both women sporting fashionable hairstyles and well-cut coats.

For most Afghans, these pictures represent a bygone Afghanistan that stands in sharp contrast to the country today, where decades of war have plunged it into a state of perpetual crisis. Today, these scenes feel like an impossible dream, a mockery of what the country has become. But that just makes it more important to show people an alternative vision of Afghanistan, Hamdard says, reminding them how much can change, not only in the past but in the present too.

IDEAS BEYOND BORDERS									INNOVATION HUB

'It's worth the risk': Afghan girls on the dreams they refuse to relinquish

Barred from school and university, Afghan girls are finding other ways to continue their education

March 23, 2022, was a dark day for girls in Afghanistan. Heart-wrenching scenes of female students crying as they were turned away from school drew sympathy from around the world, but this was only a glimpse of the suffering that ensued. Across Afghanistan, teenage girls found themselves adrift from everything that felt familiar, unable to pursue their plans and dreams. Many describe difficult days when the despair seemed insurmountable. Stuck at home, they watched their lives shrink as the Taliban tightened restrictions on women, banning them from work, university, and many public spaces.

"It was like being dead. All my sources of motivation were gone," says Arwa Wafa*, whose plans to pursue higher education were dashed when the Taliban seized power on August 15, 2021. At first, life seemed hopeless, but gradually, she realized there might be ways to salvage her future. Looking online, she enrolled in an English language course that helps students pass their TOEFL exams so they can apply for scholarships abroad.

The program, which received an Innovation Hub grant from Ideas Beyond Borders, was set up by Ghulam Reza Pazhwak to help women and girls find a way out of Afghanistan. "We have tried to create a window for girls to find another future by securing a scholarship and getting out of the country because, inside Afghanistan, we cannot see any opportunities for girls to support themselves, learn, or thrive," he says.

Here, his students share their struggles after the Taliban seized power, and their determination to recover their dreams despite the monumental challenges facing women and girls in Afghanistan.

Ideas Beyond Borders uses pseudonyms to protect the identity of our partners in Afghanistan

◉ AFGHANISTAN

Arwa Wafa*, 20

After graduating from high school, Arwa couldn't wait to embark on the next phase of her education. When that was taken, she lost her sense of self.*

I am a teenager with thousands of unfulfilled dreams living under the Taliban. I had a normal life before, but then they took over, and all my hopes were lost. I thought I would never learn again. For a while, I was severely depressed. It was like being dead; all my sources of motivation were gone. My whole focus had been on studying. I spent most of my time among books. Then, suddenly, it was forbidden to me, and countless other girls across the country. I was angry, too, because it was shameful and unfair to deny women and girls their right to education, but after a while, I realized I had to find another way to rebuild my dreams. I had thought about studying before, but now it is my primary goal. Not only that, I have my sights set on Harvard, because I want to gain the best education possible so I can bring about change in my country and improve the lives of other Afghan girls.

Anita Nikzad*, 18

An 'ocean of sadness' is how Anita describes the feeling that engulfed her when Afghanistan fell to the Taliban and she realized everything was about to change.*

I felt like I was drowning, and there was no one to save me. I couldn't walk or run or even stand. I had no strength, no power. And it got worse as the days went by and the rules grew stricter. But gradually, my outlook changed. I decided to put those terrible days behind me, accept the situation, and find a way to carry on in spite of it. These dark days are not going to last forever, but they have forced me to change my plans. Instead of studying medicine and working to support people in Afghanistan, I am studying hard to pass my TOEFL exam to secure a scholarship overseas and get my education without fear or restrictions. I am afraid of the Taliban, but if I accept their ruling on girls' education and just give up, I will always live in failure. This isn't the end of our lives, even though, for now, the situation for women in Afghanistan gets worse and worse.

Zerka Dawran*, 21

Before the Taliban seized power, Zerka Dawran was studying Law and Political Science at Kabul University, which she paid for through her work as an English instructor at the Muslim English Language Institute. Now, she is barred from both.*

"You educate a man; you educate a man. You educate a woman; you educate a generation." That's what Brigham Young, the former governor of the Utah Territory said in the nineteenth century. That's the case in Afghanistan, where women and girls, despite the multiple challenges they face, have always been eager seekers of education. Sadly, when girls get the opportunity to go to school in Afghanistan, it's only a matter of time before they get barred again. That's how it has been here for decades, and history just repeats itself. These restrictions have stolen our opportunities, killed my dreams, and made me see life in a different way.

IDEAS BEYOND BORDERS INNOVATION HUB

> "Outside, I see Taliban soldiers with their guns, flouting their dominance and intimidating people into obedience. I want to live in a society without these threats, where women can walk freely—it's worth the risk of studying to achieve that goal."

Maral Noori*, student

Maral Noori*, 19

Maral* planned to pursue a bachelor's degree in economics with the eventual aim of starting her own business before women in Afghanistan lost the right to work.

In the past 20 years, Afghan women and girls have been able to launch their own businesses and pursue successful careers thanks to education. They have held high-ranking positions, showing that their presence in the community is crucial to society. Thinking about this helps us stay strong now that those opportunities have gone and women are cut off from society. As girls, this is the worst thing that could happen to us, but the consequences will be felt by everyone. But I still want to gain an education, develop my managerial and entrepreneurial abilities, and be a business leader who can influence female participation in society. I study 20 hours a week, reading online about how to start a business and run your own company. Outside, I see Taliban soldiers with their guns, flouting their dominance and intimidating people into obedience. I want to live in a society without these threats, where women can walk freely, so it's worth the risk of studying to achieve that goal.

Sara Rezayee*, 19

Sara* was in twelfth grade, preparing for her university entrance exams with plans to study economics. Then, the Taliban seized power, and all hopes were dashed.

When the Taliban took over Afghanistan, my country became strange and unfamiliar to me. I knew that now, I would be imprisoned in my own home, deprived of my rights simply because I'm a girl. Still, I was shocked when I learned that girls would be totally barred from education. Everyone was. We didn't know what to do. Before they took over, I wanted to finish higher education and then serve my country, but now I just want to get out and escape the Taliban and their ideas. I am pursuing the TOEFL grant program in the hopes of achieving my goals abroad and becoming the successful, independent woman I have always imagined I will be. That said, I will always dream of a day when the Taliban are out of our country, and all girls are free to live the life they want.

*Ideas Beyond Borders uses pseudonyms to protect the identity of our partners in Afghanistan

◆ AFGHANISTAN

Schooling for street children in Afghanistan

Early morning classes at Hero Junior Academy give children a chance to learn while new libraries bring books to rural areas across Afghanistan

Afghan boys gather to study in the mornings before heading out to work. Image: Paeez Jahanbin

Every Friday Mustafa, 10, and Rustam, 13, get together with other boys to play a game of six-a-side at a nearby park in Kabul, Afghanistan. They are proud of their football, which was given to them brand new. "They were wrapping up cloths and sheets and making a ball out of them, so I promised I would get them a proper one," says Ahmad Jawid Karimyan, who runs an informal school for these boys when they aren't working during the week.

Lessons last three hours a day, which is all the children can spare. They study from 7 am to 10 am and then work until seven or eight in the evening, polishing shoes, washing cars, and selling plastic bags on the streets. "Some of them are beggars. They need this income to survive," says Karimyan, who set up Hero Junior Academy in 2022 to provide access to learning for Afghan street children who are missing out on school.

Initially, many refused to attend because they needed the time to earn, so Karimyan offered to provide breakfast. "The goal was to bring kids without parents or guardians, who are doing child labor, and give them the tools to learn," he adds. Supported by an Innovation Hub grant from Ideas Beyond Borders, he hired teachers to run classes in Maths, English, and Dari, the form of Persian spoken in Afghanistan. This is Mustafa and Rustam's favorite class because, like many of their classmates, they are unable to read and write. "We want to be able to read storybooks," Mustafa says.

Over time, the emphasis on breakfast has subsided as the boy's appetite for learning increases. "Even on days when we run out of gas to cook food, they are happy just to eat bread and learn," Karimyan says. Most hadn't considered education before joining Hero Junior Academy, which launched earlier this

Ahmad Jawid Karimyan with students at Ghorband Library. He believes reading and knowledge are the paths to tackling the radical ideologies and oppressive social structures that curtail people's freedom in Afghanistan. Image: Paeez Jahanbin

year. "Many of them thought they would be polishing shoes for the rest of their lives. That was how they saw the world and their place in it," says Karimyan.

He knows from experience what that vision of the future feels like. As a child, he missed out on school to work on the streets, selling water and ferrying goods in exchange for small sums. "I really loved reading books, but I had no money to buy them, and there were many others like me," he says.

When the Taliban seized power in August 2021, Afghanistan suffered an economic collapse that pushed almost the entire population into poverty. Today, the streets of Kabul are lined with beggars, many of them children whose families are unable to buy food amid soaring prices. Outside the capital, the situation is even worse as rural areas that have been sidelined for years fall deeper into poverty.

Last year, Karimyan launched a library in Ghorband, a district of Parwan Province that sits in the foothills of the Hindu Kush mountain range, about two hours by car from Kabul. Life in this part of Afghanistan was hard even before the economic turmoil of the past two years. Recent decades have seen very little investment in Ghorband, a rural area where fertile plains produce a rich crop of almonds, apples, grapes, apricots, and peaches, fed by meltwater running off the Shibar Pass.

In photographs, it looks idyllic, with the clear waters of the Ghorband River winding through a leafy valley framed by snow-capped mountains reaching toward blue skies. But the picture is very different in the towns and villages of Parwan, where lack of investment has fuelled illiteracy and unemployment, leaving more than half the population aged seven or older without any formal education.

"Access to education is bad across many rural areas in Afghanistan, and Ghorband is no exception," Karimyan says. "During the sixties and seventies, they would bring portable cinemas and books fairs. They even built a school. But during the republic, all they did was modernize the roads."

The library was the first to open in Ghorband in over 50 years, and he has since opened others in three more provinces—Badakhshan, Takhar, and

Ahmad Jawid Karimyan is opening libraries in rural areas across Afghanistan. Images: Paeez Jahanbin

Paktia. "At first, people were confused by the concept, but once we explained how the libraries work, we saw how eager they were to use the books and learn," says Karimyan.

Ghorband Library, which was funded by an earlier Innovation Hub grant from Ideas Beyond Borders, now houses around 1,500 books and welcomes over 100 visitors a day. Many take books home to their sisters, wives, and mothers, who can't come in person due to current restrictions on women in Afghanistan.

"I wanted to create a space for the kids who work on the streets to show them that this, in Ghorband, is not the whole world. Now I am at a point where I cannot stop what I'm doing; people around me are interested, their families are interested," says Karimyan. "When I go there and see their faces, their enthusiasm to learn or study, their progress, it compels me to work harder for them because I see that this is a necessity now."

His next step is to secure funding to purchase a few computers so he can teach the children IT skills, which they are keen to learn. Watching the transformation has been remarkable, Karimyan says, and he hopes to expand the academy to other areas of Afghanistan where child labor is on the rise. "These kids thought they would be polishing shoes for the rest of their lives. That was how they saw the world and their future. Now, they have bigger dreams and a motivation to continue their education. They are hopeful," he says.

"The goal was to bring kids without parents or guardians, who are doing child labor, and give them the tools to learn. Even on days when we run out of gas to cook food, they are happy just to eat bread and learn."

Ahmad Jawid Karimyan
Founder of Hero Junior Academy

◉ AFGHANISTAN

The Sun's Daughter: A story of hope

The future looks bleak for Afghan children, but books remind them that stories can change and there is room for hope even in the darkest times

The story begins with a town deep in the mountains of Afghanistan. There is no daylight in this town; it is always night. The people here are used to living this way. Long ago, a demon came and stole their sun, so the flowers died, and the birds left, leaving them with perpetual winter.

In Hazaristan, the remote mountain region of Afghanistan where the story is set, winters are harsh, and life is difficult, so people relate to this old folk tale and the predicament it presents. Children listening to the tale gasp in awe as they hear of a girl with golden hair who confronts the demon and restores light to her people.

In a deeply patriarchal society, it's inspiring for young girls to see a female protagonist portrayed as the hero, says K.H Rasa, who worked with a children's author and illustrator to produce the book version of this old Hazara folktale. "This story is very relevant at the moment as people struggle for their freedom and rights but find there is darkness blocking their access to knowledge," he says.

For girls who were barred from secondary school in Afghanistan when the Taliban came to power in August 2021, the story is particularly resonant. "It gives them hope for the future," says Rasa, who oversees the Afghanistan Box Library Extension program (ABLE), which was set up to promote a culture of reading and establish small libraries in schools and communities across Afghanistan,

Each year, the project publishes between 20 and 25 storybooks for children in Farsi/Dari, Pashto, and Uzbeki, Afghanistan's three main languages, distrib-

> *"Every child has a dream here, and they should go to school to get knowledge and change their world, but right now they just see that everything has collapsed overnight, and they need a reason to have hope for the future."*

K.H. Rasa
Manager of the Afghanistan Box Library
Extension program at ACKU

ABLE distributes books to children in marginalized communities across Afghanistan. Image: Paeez Jahanbin

uting over 50,000 copies around the country. They focus on reaching marginalized children in orphanages and under-represented communities where access to books is extremely limited. "Children's literature is not a well-known genre in Afghan communities; most children here don't have access to reading material other than textbooks," Rasa says.

Fourteen years after the project launched, Rasa's team has published over 450 easy–to–read titles for different age groups, newly literate people, and adults. This includes a collection of 280 personal stories chronicling people's experiences during the COVID-19 pandemic. However, in the past two years, Afghanistan's economic collapse has starved the project of funds, and the publication program has ground to a halt.

When Rasa heard about the Ideas Beyond Borders Innovation Hub, he applied immediately and secured a grant to commission and publish a beautifully illustrated version of The Sun's Daughter and the Black Demon by well-known Afghan children's author M.H. Mohammadi. "Even if we can produce a single storybook for children in need, it means a lot," says Rasa. "If we cannot provide children with materials to learn and develop ideas, they will remain isolated with nothing to inspire them or provide a positive message for the future."

This is particularly true now, with Afghanistan on the brink of economic collapse as the population endures its second year of Taliban rule. For the marginalized children that ABLE focuses on—those from minority and disadvantaged backgrounds who may be orphans, suffer from disabilities, or are affected by child labor, drugs, and other crime, books like this are a rare resource.

"Every child has a dream here, and they should go to school to get knowledge and change their world, but right now, they just see that everything has collapsed overnight, and they need a reason to have hope for the future," Rasa says. It may just be a story, but stories have the power to inspire change, and he hopes that these young readers will see an opportunity to triumph in the tale of the sun's daughter as she banishes the demon and restores light to her world.

◆ AFGHANISTAN

Tech opportunities for Afghan talent

Inspirand is opening the Canadian market to IT experts in Afghanistan

Samiullah Nazari wants to raise the profile of Afghan talent among overseas employers

It was frustrating, scrolling through job listings he couldn't apply for. After seven years as a software engineer and web designer, Samiullah Nazari was an ideal candidate for the digital design and development projects posted on international forums. But none of these companies would consider taking on a freelancer in Afghanistan. "It was a real struggle, I saw there were projects I could do, but there was no connection to the international markets. We simply don't have access," he says.

The problem was payments. Paypal and other online transfer mechanisms are not available in Afghanistan, making it difficult to get money to Afghans from abroad. The virtual collapse of the banking system since the Taliban takeover and the economic crisis that followed left people like Nazari in greater need of freelance work from abroad but unable to apply for the roles. "I had a few friends in the industry who got work through relatives abroad, but not everyone is going to do that for you because it's a real hassle," he says.

This approach is convoluted and requires relatives to set up an account to receive the payment on their behalf. They send the money to the recipient in Afghanistan through the hawala system, an informal method of transferring money through a network of money brokers across the country. Hawala transfers, which operate without the physical movement of money, are widely used in Afghanistan, but not many people have an overseas relative able or willing to do this. "So people with excellent skillsets are unable to take on work because they can't get paid," Nazari says.

In January 2022, he moved to Canada and realized he could share the opportunity with others back in Afghanistan. His plan was simple—set up a company to take on web design, development, and branding projects in Canada, then outsource

> *"There's no lack of talent in Afghanistan, but there is a lack of avenues for the global market to access it. Inspirand is one of many innovative solutions which is leveling the playing field, allowing everyone to access the same opportunities."*

Faisal Al Mutar
President of Ideas Beyond Borders

the work to freelancers in Afghanistan. They would be paid in Canadian dollars, substantially boosting their income thanks to the exchange rate, while the lower rates they charge would help secure work in the competitive Canadian market.

"There are so many projects Afghans can do here. I want to bring Canadian opportunities to them," he says, pointing to the relative value of a foreign wage in Afghanistan, where the money goes substantially further than in Toronto, where he is now based. "A thousand Canadian dollars might cover a few weeks' rent on a one-bedroom apartment here, but in Afghanistan, it would support a family of five or more in a large house for at least a month."

Nazari launched Inspirand in November 2022 with funding from an Ideas Beyond Borders Innovation Hub grant. "It was early in the morning when I received the email confirming the grant. I won't forget that moment," he says. For IBB, Inspirand offers enormous potential to help talented young people in Afghanistan build sustainable careers in an incredibly challenging environment.

"There's no lack of talent in Afghanistan, but there is a lack of avenues for the global market to access it. Inspirand is one of many innovative solutions which are leveling the playing field, allowing everyone to access the same opportunities," says Faisal Al Mutar, President of Ideas Beyond Borders.

Nazari hopes that gaining work experience with international companies will help the freelancers he employs secure more roles in the future and plans to take people on full-time when he has a steady flow of work coming in. "The situation in Afghanistan is terrible at the moment, but by building a bridge between these two markets, we can create the access and eligibility people need to get hired and eventually find a way out."

◉ AFGHANISTAN

A way forward for women in Afghanistan

The project helping Afghan women build businesses and reclaim their futures under Taliban rule

Afghan women learn new skills on courses run by Empower Her Craft

At first, the dreams Zara* had cherished felt like a mockery as she considered her future. She was mid-way through a degree in Business and Administration, hoping one day to launch her own company, when the Taliban seized power in Afghanistan. It quickly became clear that the new regime would never allow her to stay at university and pursue the life she had planned.

Around her, friends and relatives went from shock to grief to despair as the ban on female education was followed by strict restrictions on employment, cutting women off from all but a few careers. Further rulings soon followed, barring them from many public spaces. Stuck inside, there was nothing to distract Zara from the hopelessness that grew each day.

Two and a half years later, the outlook remains bleak, but she refuses to give up. As the initial shock subsided, she searched for new opportunities, aware that some women were finding different ways to pursue their goals, even under the watchful eye of the regime. "I heard a lot of stories about the Taliban in the nineties, and I was so afraid when they came to Kabul," the 21-year-old says. "But there's a little more space these days. We can at least work from home."

This small space is where activists like Ahmad Shekib Sarwary focus their efforts to forge new opportunities for women under the Taliban. Last year, the former youth leader set up Empower Her Craft, a project that teaches women handicrafts so that they can sell products online. "After the collapse of the previous government, the situation became very bad for women, and we wanted to help," says Sarwary. "This program gives women the opportunity to go out and do something positive with their lives. It's a hopeful project for them in the midst of all the frustrations."

Prior to the Taliban takeover, Sarwary hosted students in cultural camps around Afghanistan and ran trips to neighboring Uzbekistan. Juggling an active involvement in youth projects with his university degree kept Sarwary busy, but the collapse of the government put a stop to this work. Now, he focuses his energy on training women, inspired by the response he has received from participants, who have already sold several items to buyers in Australia and New Zealand.

It's a positive start, and Sarwary is optimistic that the demand for high-quality Afghan handicrafts domestically and abroad will give women a chance to support their families without attracting the attention of Taliban officials. Handicraft projects like this are permissible, he says, because they are not directly linked to education, and women can work from home. "So long as genders remain segregated and there are no men on-site, they don't have a problem with us," he adds.

Watching the women's progress is inspiring, but the project can only help a fraction of those who have been denied the lives they deserve. "The sad story is that there are many more women out there who are unable to access these opportunities and find work," Sarwary says. To young people like him, the last few years have felt like a cruel nightmare, springing from another era. "So much has changed. We were used to freedom, to expressing our ideas and doing as we pleased. Now, so many things are forced on us by outsiders telling us what to do. We're at home, but it doesn't feel like home at all."

The Taliban has been swift to roll back women's rights in Afghanistan, condemning a new generation to suffer the same oppression as their mothers under the first brutal regime. Within months of seizing power in August 2021, a series of new rulings had dismantled the gains of recent decades, which saw a rise in female education and employment. The difference, now, is that more Afghan women are educated and refuse to be condemned to a life behind closed doors.

Women like Zara, who has resumed her university studies online and joined Empower Her Craft to learn new skills and launch her own enterprise. While not the future she envisaged, it is a path to independence and a chance to fill her days with productive employment. "I'm still hopeless and frustrated, but now at least we can work from home. I plan to work on my skills, be independent, and run my own business," she says.

She is one of 30 women participating in the project, using Innovation Hub funding to teach tailoring, embroidery, glasswork, and other skills to allow women to produce their own products to sell from home or online. The primary aim is to help women find a new career path and secure a reliable income that supports themselves and their families at a time when many people have lost their jobs in Afghanistan.

"We cannot change the restrictions or stop the human rights violations taking place under this despotic regime," says Faisal Al Mutar, President of Ideas Beyond Borders. "What we can do, is help women access opportunities and achieve their potential by supporting courageous people like Ahmad, who is finding new ways for women to thrive, even in these difficult times."

It is one of numerous projects operating with IBB support in Afghanistan, where the Taliban has stifled free expression, banned women from education, and re-written school curriculums to enforce their dogmatic beliefs. "Now more than ever, young people need to know that there is a world beyond Afghanistan. That's why IBB is supporting organizations that provide young people with access to reading materials, from libraries and underground schools to lessons and workshops designed to support a love of learning through the written word," Al Mutar adds.

Once the women at Empower Her Craft have mastered new skills, a second part of the project will help them create a retail space and launch their products online. It's one of the few avenues left open to women like Khadija*, who had ambitions to become a journalist. "I wanted to be a news reporter or television host and share the truth," says the 20-year-old, who was forced to leave school before taking her university entrance exams. "I wanted to be a role model and inspire other girls."

There is a strong sense of camaraderie among women on the course. All have suffered the loss of their dreams and have been forced to accept an unthinkable reality. Sara* was in the final year of an economics degree when she had to give up her studies. For a while, she could only despair at the loss of the life she had worked towards. "I became depressed, but I didn't want to lose hope," she says.

The only way ahead was to launch a small business, so she started to get involved in handicrafts. "When I came across the Innovation Hub and realized I could help other women learn these skills and set up their own business, I saw the potential to make a real impact," says Sara, who became program manager at Empower Her Craft after calling on her own creative skills to find a way through the crisis.

Her plan now is to help other Afghan women find hope and forge new futures by redirecting their talents. "I want to show the world that Afghan women will find ways to work, create, and do amazing things, even with these restrictions," she says. "Our women have strong hearts, and that is all it takes for us to keep going."

Ideas Beyond Borders uses pseudonyms to protect the identity of our partners in Afghanistan

📍 LEBANON

Lebanon

Living in Lebanon

The northern Lebanese city of Tripoli was once a beautiful place. Noisy roads, now choked with traffic, began as spacious boulevards, where palms rustled in the coastal breeze and citrus trees sent aromas of orange blossom through the streets. Ornate fountains cooled the air in sun-soaked squares, and the shaded medina bustled with life as vendors hawked soap, sweets, and handicrafts in the city's famous souqs.

It's in these winding alleyways that the last vestiges of Tripoli's illustrious past still lingers, as old men tell of better times, pointing out medieval khans and caravanserai that whisper stories from across the centuries.

As a child, Issam Fawaz was proud to call this home. Tucked between snow-capped mountains and cobalt seas, Tripoli's strategic location and natural port made it a historic hub for trade, leaving a legacy of progress and prosperity as the city grew. Growing up in the nineties, this felt like a good place to live. Alongside the historic treasures, it had modern infrastructure and some of the best facilities in the country. "Tripoli was way better back then. The economy was booming, and we had good schools, hospitals, and public services," Fawaz, 36, recalls.

A few decades later, he hardly recognizes the city he grew up in. Marginalized and maligned, it has long been sidelined by central government, but the latest financial crisis has exacerbated its woes. Today, Tripoli is a microcosm of the problems facing Lebanon, subsumed in the conflict, corruption, and political failures that have brought the country to the brink of collapse.

It is the poorest city on the Mediterranean coast, dotted with slums and refugee camps, where families cram into single-room shacks and survive off scraps with two hours of electricity a day. Areas that used to be beautiful, like the coastal community of Mina, with its white-washed houses and lamp-lit

INNOVATION HUB

Rasha Abdul-Hussein Shukr and Nahida Ali Tawbe established Atelier Hartouka to provide employment to female artisans. Image: Natheer Halawani

streets, have fallen prey to the poverty engulfing the city. The old medina, still the finest example of Mamluk architecture outside Egypt, should be a UNESCO World Heritage site, but it has fallen too far into disrepair.

Rising tensions

The decline in living conditions has contributed to a social shift in Tripoli as mistrust and hostility brews between religious communities once more. At Fawaz's school in the nineties, Christian and Muslim children mingled in class, part of a new generation that was moving beyond the religious hostilities of the civil war years. "Now the level of tolerance is reversing and we're back to hearing that this guy is Alawite or that woman is Christian," he says.

Fear of antagonizing certain sects stifles free expression in Lebanon, leaving a vacuum for radical ideologies to converge. "I was born towards the end of the war, and growing up, we knew what it meant," Fawaz says, describing the bitter sectarian conflict that splintered the country from 1975 to 1990. "After that, people were more open-minded, but young people now don't remember the pain of that time. They are being radicalized without knowing where it could take them."

He joined Ideas Beyond Borders in 2019, hoping to address the problems that led to Tripoli's decline and towns and cities like it across the Middle East. Working across multiple programs, including the Innovation Hub, he sees the benefits these grants bring to the city. "It gives people hope, a way forward, so they can think about creating a better future," he says.

Currency crash

Today, Tripoli's wealth is concentrated in the hands of a powerful few who rule through a system of patronage, distributing jobs and services in exchange for political support. It's a model employed throughout Lebanon, where a self-serving elite has exploited sectarian divisions to pillage public finances, shoring up power and lining their pockets at the expense of much-needed reform.

The result of this corruption and economic mismanagement is the country's worst financial crisis since the 1850s. Calls to implement reforms and unlock international aid to assist the country's recovery have failed, leaving its beleaguered population to pay the price. After five years of consecutive crises, Lebanon's middle class has all but vanished, pushed into poverty or fled overseas amid a currency crash that collapsed the banking system, dissolved people's savings, and destroyed their livelihoods.

Today, more than 80 percent of people in Lebanon live below the poverty line, victims of what the World Bank has described as, "a deliberate depression…orchestrated by (an) elite that has long captured the state and lived off its economic rents."

The downturn began in 2019 when the effects of this financial mismanagement could no longer be held at arm's length. Gulf investment had dried up as non-state actors gained influence on the country's political scene, and desperate strategies to balance the budget only worked in the short term. Rather than tax the wealthy to repay foreign loans, the government imposed a fee on WhatsApp calls, prompting mass demonstrations as a frustrated population demanded wholesale reform. The state's finances, described by some as a giant Ponzi scheme, collapsed, as the currency slid from 1,500 to the dollar before the crisis to about 23,000 in January 2022.

More than two years later, Lebanon is still without a government as rival parties protect vested interests and hinder recovery to shore up support.

Another Lebanon

Other crises have compounded the situation. In 2020, the Covid pandemic hit, causing widespread food shortages and deepening the country's financial woes. Then, in August of that year, the Beirut port explosion devastated swathes of the city, killing 218 people and symbolizing once again the destruction

IDEAS BEYOND BORDERS									INNOVATION HUB

An aerial view showing Tripoli's historic architecture.
Image: Shutterstock

A fruit seller in the narrow streets of Tripoli. Image: Shutterstock

LEBANON

"We are fighting to keep cultural liberty and freedom of expression. If the war happens, many more will leave, and the fanatics will take over."

Micheline Abukhater
Founder of jewelry brand
Light of Beirut

wrought by a corrupt ruling class. In 2024, with Hezbollah and Israel exchanging fire across the country's southern border, the Lebanese wait to see whether the bombardment of Gaza will draw them into another war. For many of those who haven't already left, this would be the final straw.

Some, however, refuse to go. Innovation Hub grantee Micheline Abukhater is a history-teacher-turned- jewelry-designer whose work celebrates a time when Lebanon's diverse communities lived more peacefully. "The essence of Lebanon comes from its different communities — it has always been a melting pot of people and cultures," she says. "So many people are leaving. If I go, another little bit of this country's culture will vanish with me."

She draws inspiration from Lebanon's 1960s heyday when Beirut was know as the Paris of the Middle East. Back then, it was a hotspot for film stars and royalty, renowned for its glamorous clubs and luxurious hotels. "Before the war, people came from all over the world to enjoy our way of life—to go from the beach to the mountains in an hour, enjoy good Mediterranean food, and soak up the sunshine," Abukhater recalls. As another conflict looms, she worries that the last vestiges of this era will vanish forever. "We are fighting to keep cultural liberty and freedom of expression. If the war happens, many more will leave, and the fanatics will take over," she says.

Preventable problems

The roots of the religious divisions that have paralyzed the political process in Lebanon can be traced back to the aftermath of the war when spoils were divvied up, and influence was allocated along sectarian lines. Intended to establish peace, the Taif Accords of November 1989 decreed that power would be split, with a President from the Maronite Christian community, a Sunni Prime Minister, and a Shi'ite Muslim as the Speaker of Parliament. It ended the war but perpetuated old divisions, leaving space for external actors to stoke tensions through proxy forces, which flared once more when uprisings broke out across the Middle East in 2011.

In Tripoli, old religious tensions erupted into open gunfire between rival neighborhoods on either side of Syria Street. These days, it doesn't take much to provoke conflict in this part of the city, where bomb-blasted facades and bullet-pocked buildings are a constant reminder of the violence that hovers overhead. Grinding poverty in the Alawite neighborhood of Jabal Mohsen and Sunni Bab al-Tabbaneh have made them easy targets for war-lords-turned-politicians, who inflame hostilities to shore up support.

There's little else to occupy youth in these marginalized communities. Unemployment is rampant, making them fertile recruiting grounds for ISIS, who lure desperate young men across the border with the promise of regular salaries in Syria or Iraq. This has given Tripoli a reputation as a hotbed of extremism, but amid deepening poverty, lack of basic services, and arbitrary arrests that brand young men as terrorists, what's missing is the opportunity to find a way out.

"This is what scares me; it's become a place that offers no hope," says Fawaz. "What are those terrorists but people who have lost hope? I'm not talking about their evil leaders, but the thousands of people fooled and brainwashed into joining. This is something we can prevent."

Repairing the damage

Through his work at Ideas Beyond Borders, Fawaz sees the impact of creating opportunities in sidelined communities across the Middle East. But it's in Lebanon that he feels the significance of supporting these projects most keenly and watches the benefits unfold. "I see the change in their projects after receiving the grant. It is giving hope to people who have been abandoned by their community, their government, and sometimes even by their friends and families," he says.

Recent grants have supported projects that provide employment opportunities, like Atelier Hartouka, a Beirut boutique that commissions women in vulnerable communities to produce handcrafted clothes, bags, and accessories. It's a big responsibility for owners Rasha Abdul-Hussein Shukr and Nahida Ali Tawbe, who left their jobs in the NGO sector to found the business. "They rely on us for work. There's nothing else out there," Tawbe says.

With the war in Gaza encroaching further across Lebanon's border, business in the country has been on hold, and profits are down. Thanks to an Innovation Hub grant, the atelier was able to support 20 women with new commissions, but it's difficult to keep going in this climate. "Every time the situation improves, something major happens, and it gets worse," Shukr says. What motivates them is the responsibility they feel towards these women and the sense that they are part of the solution. "It is small business that will rebuild the country," Shukr adds.

At Ideas Beyond Borders, a growing proportion of Innovation Hub funding is being allocated to startups, small businesses, and social enterprises that provide jobs and invigorate the economy, restoring the promise of progress in a seemingly hopeless world. Many Lebanese now live day by day with survival as their only real goal. These success stories show that there are opportunities out there, even as the crisis deepens and the country plunges to new lows.

"By giving people the opportunity to create something for themselves, it gives them hope that they can survive in their own country. Not only that, but they can be productive, and help others be productive too," Fawaz says. This, for him, is what makes the Innovation Hub's work so instrumental in carving out a better future for Lebanon. "It doesn't only help those who receive the grant but opens up opportunities for others around them as well. It creates that social connection needed to repair the damage and restore some of the hope and harmony we have lost in the past five years."

"By giving people the opportunity to create something for themselves, it gives them hope that they can survive in their own country. Not only that, but they can be productive, and help others be productive too."

Issam Fawaz
Lebanon advisor and data and communication manager at Ideas Beyond Borders

● LEBANON

An economy ravaged by crises turns to small businesses to rebuild the country

Profits have plummeted since the start of the war in Gaza, piling more pressure on Lebanon's small business owners as they fight to stay afloat

Weekends are usually busy at Atelier Hartouka, a popular boutique just around the corner from Beirut's fashionable Badaro district. Before the war in Gaza, it was a place Lebanese socialites frequented, rubbing shoulders with foreign shoppers as they browsed hand-made bags and embroidered jackets. "Our clothes are one-offs—people know they won't walk out and bump into someone else wearing the same piece," says Rasha Abdul-Hussein Shukr, who has built Atelier Hartouka into a successful social enterprise with her colleague Nahida Ali Tawbe, 46.

When it opened in 2018, the boutique employed just three women to make their clothes, bags, and accessories by hand. Five years later, they have 45 women on their books, many of whom live in refugee camps or low-income neighborhoods, where employment opportunities, particularly for women, are scarce. "We give them the raw materials, and they do the work from home," Shukr, 37, explains.

Working in the NGO sector for over ten years, she and Tawbe saw firsthand the limitations of traditional empowerment programs for women, which taught technical skills like sewing and embroidery but failed to provide jobs afterward. They set up Atelier Hartouka to complement this vocational training and provide female artisans with regular commissions. "They rely on us for work. There's nothing else out there," Tawbe says.

Five years of consecutive crises have ravaged the Lebanese economy, hitting low-income communities the hardest. Currency devaluation and skyrocketing inflation contributed to the collapse of the banking system, fuelling unemployment and pushing many workers to seek opportunities abroad. Then, the

Linda Nasser specializes in crochet work, producing beautiful pieces for Atelier Hartouka. Image: Natheer Halawani

♦ LEBANON

01 Lana Wejhani is a Syrian jewelry maker and produces accessories for Atelier Hartouka. Image: Natheer Halawani

02 Atika Abbas is an Iraqi artisan specializing in intricate embroidery work. Image: Natheer Halawani

03 Fiza Ezzedine is Lebanese and uses her crochet skills to make peg dolls. Image: Natheer Halawani

04 Najah Abdallah is from Lebanon and produces patchwork designs for the boutique. Image: Natheer Halawani

COVID-19 crisis hit and ushered in a fresh round of financial woes as businesses closed and food shortages spread. As vast swathes of the population sank below the poverty line, a massive blast at Beirut port shook the city in August 2020, reinforcing the failures of a corrupt ruling class that has prioritized self-enrichment at the expense of the state.

With foreign rescue packages contingent on reforms that fail to materialize and the government frozen in political stalemate, progress must come from within. "We believe in a circular economy—it is small business that will rebuild the country," Shukr says.

Local enterprise provides employment, bolsters the private sector, and enables people to confront these challenges themselves, which is why Ideas Beyond Borders supports businesses like Atelier Hartouka. "This isn't about fixing Lebanon's problems by launching another new program and injecting it with cash. It's about empowering ordinary people with small sums to implement sustainable solutions that impact entire communities, says Faisal Al Mutar, President of Ideas Beyond Borders.

In 2021, Shukr and Tawbe quit their jobs in the non-profit sector to focus full-time on expanding Atelier Hartouka and the number of vulnerable female artisans it supports. Last October, they placed their orders for the winter season ahead, anticipating the usual uplift in sales over the festive period. Three months on, they are going over their figures in despair. Days after finalizing their winter stock list, Hamas launched its gruesome attack on Israel, and a terrifying retaliation ensued as Israeli forces began a relentless bombardment of the Gaza strip that has killed over 34,000 Palestinians to date. Lebanon has hovered on the brink of war ever since.

"In this harsh climate, we are hardly able to sustain the business. Our cause and mission is to support the women, but now people have stopped buying," says Tawbe. A month into the war, their sales were down by 85 percent. As Christmas approached, they saw a 50 percent drop compared to previous years, at what should be one of the busiest times of the year. The result was a vastly reduced budget for new materials and fewer commissions to sustain

05. Atelier Hartouka. Image: Natheer Halawani

06. Fadia Al-Ahmad is from Syria and works as a seamstress for Atelier Hartouka. Image: Natheer Halawani

the women—at a time when there is little support for Lebanon's poorest. "It's a huge burden, we feel responsible for them," Tawbe adds.

Across Lebanon, businesses have ground to a halt. Cafes and restaurants that once bustled with guests now stand empty as people wait for a war that feels increasingly likely as Hezbollah trade strikes across the border with Israel. The United Nations Development Programme (UNDP) has warned that Lebanon stands to lose up to four percent of its GDP due to the ongoing war in Gaza. "Every day we are witnessing the profound impacts of the conflict on the lives and livelihoods of the people of South Lebanon and beyond," said Melanie Hauenstein, Resident Representative, Lebanon, UNDP, pointing to the need for "immediate socio-economic and livelihood support" to sustain vulnerable communities.

Social enterprises like Atelier Hartouka do this every day, but with sales down, they are struggling to maintain momentum. "It was really stressful up to mid-November, but then we decided to do something about it," says Shukr. Together, they re-activated the boutique's social media page and redoubled efforts to boost sales. With increased capacity and investment, they could expand online and tap into foreign markets, but for now, they are focused on staying afloat.

An Innovation Hub grant from Ideas Beyond Borders has come at the right time, allowing them to provide 20 women with new commissions. "The grant helped us support the most vulnerable women we work with. A $100 or $150 commission is a big boost in this climate. They were really happy," Shukr adds.

One of the women is Najah, a widow and a single mother who uses the money from sewing commissions to put her daughter through university. Another is Fadia, who needs urgent surgery to remove a cyst on her uterus. As a Syrian, she receives little help from NGOs, whose funding to support refugees in Lebanon has largely dried up. "We put a plan together for her to secure the amount needed by taking on additional work to afford the surgery. There are many stories like this," says Tawbe.

Many of her friends have left Lebanon, weary of trying to rebuild their lives in a climate of perpetual crisis. "Every time the situation improves, something major happens, and it gets worse," Shukr says. But both agree they will remain in the country. "Of course, we will stay till the end. We have the ladies to think of, and despite everything, we believe in Lebanon."

IDEAS BEYOND BORDERS INNOVATION HUB

The code to success: Lebanese youth retrain in tech

SE Factory runs coding boot camps that give Lebanese students the skills they need to secure employment in the technology sector

SE Factory has an 85 percent employment rate for its alumni. Image: Natheer Halawani

Finding a table in one of Beirut's crowded cafes is difficult. Finding one next to a plug socket is virtually impossible. The ongoing economic crisis that has gripped Lebanon since 2019 has exacerbated the country's electricity problems, with power outages that last up to 22 hours a day in most regions. For many, cafes are now the only place they can study or work.

"A lot of our students couldn't connect online at home, so they had to go to cafes—but cafes across the country were overwhelmed with people trying to connect and charge their phones and laptops," says Zeina Saab, co-founder of SE Factory, a social enterprise that teaches tech skills to unemployed youth. The organization has a dedicated workspace in Beirut Digital District, but few students can now afford the fuel to get there, she adds.

SE Factory runs coding bootcamps in Lebanon, with a focus on providing access to training for underprivileged youth. The organization has a 90 percent employment rate for students that complete the course, with one recent graduate securing a job at Microsoft on a salary of US $4,000 a month, but the situation in Lebanon is forcing many young people to reconsider their study plans.

LEBANON

The impact of the currency crash, scarce job opportunities, and ongoing political deadlock present few prospects for Lebanese youth trying to carve out a future amid multiple crises. "First, we had the revolution, which, while a great step for our country, put our programs on hold for many weeks. Then it was COVID-19, economic collapse, and the Beirut port blast with the political stagnation that followed," says Saab.

But, amid all of these setbacks, it was poor access to electricity that hindered SE Factory students from completing their course.

So, when the team received an Innovation Hub grant from Ideas Beyond Borders, they used it to purchase 13 power banks, allowing students to work remotely around the country. "We offered them to students that needed them the most so they were able to work from home comfortably… If it weren't for that support, they would have had to drop out," Saab says.

The course is free but graduates are expected to pay a fee after they get hired, says Saab, who launched SE Factory in 2016 with co-founder Fadi Bizri after identifying the need for qualified coders in Lebanon and globally, despite thousands of computer science students graduating in the country every year. Companies in the SE Factory network also pay a fee to recruit from the graduate pool.

"The demand for coding is not going down. It's critical for the way we function on a daily basis. Everything requires this key skill, and everything is technology-based, and that's not going away," she says.

"The current economic crisis may be devastating, but SE Factory embodies the spirit of Lebanese resilience. They are empowering both locals and refugees with the skill sets needed to survive in the modern global economy," says Faisal Al Mutar, President of Ideas Beyond Borders.

A few months after receiving the power banks, most students had completed the course and secured employment, passing them on to the next cohort. "We've been able to find companies abroad desperate for the talent we're creating, and the fact they are ready to pay us a fee shows the quality we are providing them," Saab says.

It's not just computer science students that take SE Factory courses, which include a six-week part-time foundation course and the signature Fullstack Web Development program, which runs for 14 weeks. "We are seeing bio majors and finance majors with zero background in this come here and become coders," Saab says. Once, these students might have gone into the education or banking sectors, but with teacher salaries depleted by the devaluation of the Lebanese currency and the country's banking system in a state of collapse, they are turning to coding.

To date, the government has done very little to promote the sector but the country is full of eager, ambitious youth who just need new skills, says Saab, who believes coding should be taught from a young age in Lebanese schools and is planning to collaborate with other tech training initiatives across Lebanon to turn the country into a hub for tech talent. "We've seen successful models in Eastern Europe, India, and Pakistan, where these countries nurtured thousands of coders and became the place to be for companies. That's the vision we have for Lebanon," she says.

Word of the SE Factory boot camps has spread, and the team has had to double the number of coding boot camps it runs each year to meet demand. The next step is to introduce a data engineering course in the fall, tapping into another gap in the job market by training youth to meet demand. "COVID-19 taught us that we can learn and work online, so even if not many of the job opportunities are coming from Lebanon, a lot are coming from abroad, which also gives hope for these youth that not all doors are closed in their faces," Saab says.

The remote opportunities enable students to stay in Lebanon and earn US dollars, helping to reverse the brain drain as thousands of youth pursue opportunities abroad. "There are so many young people in the country out of work, desperate for a job, and a huge demand for coding globally, so there is a clear gap that can be filled," Saab says.

IDEAS BEYOND BORDERS · INNOVATION HUB

Pendants and peace: Lebanese designer draws from the past

At a historic mosque in the Lebanese city of Tyre, Micheline Abukhater discovered a motif that inspired her to celebrate culture through colorful designs

01. Micheline Abukhater.
Image: Natheer Halawani

02. Bracelets featuring the brand's signature star motif.
Image: Natheer Halawani

Micheline Abukhater never imagined her jewelry designs would go viral. When she started selling hand-made pieces at the Sursock Museum in Beirut, she thought people might appreciate their cultural significance, and maybe a few would make a purchase. Now, everywhere she goes, she sees the 10-point star set in colored tiles, which has become ubiquitous in fashion, art, and design around the world.

Few know it started with a history teacher in Lebanon. "Friends thought I was crazy, but then people took it and put it everywhere," she says.

Abukhater didn't copyright the design, but she's happy to see it spread. For her, the motive was never to make money. Instead, she wanted to express a wish that one day Lebanon would achieve the harmony embodied by this symbol, which recalls a time when different communities lived peacefully side by side, before civil war splintered relations between the country's 18 sects.

Abukhater discovered the star's heritage on a trip to southern Lebanon, when she took her students to Tyre, an ancient port city on the Levantine coast. Though predominantly Shia Muslim, Tyre has long had a sizeable Christian minority and was once home to a large Jewish community. Touring the old mosque, Abukhater learned from their guide that it was once a synagogue, and the decorative tiles were designed by Jewish artisans.

"The Jews would design them, the Christians made them, and the Muslims sold them—everyone worked together," she says.

LEBANON

One of the world's oldest continually inhabited cities, Tyre was founded in the Bronze Age by the Phoenicians, a Semitic-speaking people who lived along the coast of modern-day Syria, Lebanon, and northern Israel. Tyre grew to become the hub for their trading empire before passing to the Persians and later the Greeks. Under Roman rule, it became a center for Christianity before the Islamic conquest in the seventh century marked a new era in its history. As a busy trading post and thriving port city, it has always drawn people of diverse cultures and communities, including a sizeable Jewish community, whose presence there dates back to biblical times.

Today, most of Lebanon's Jewish community is long gone, and the Christian population is dwindling as the country teeters on the edge of collapse. Abukhater was tempted to leave after losing her house, her car, and many possessions during the Beirut port blast in 2020, but finds she cannot abandon her country. "The essence of Lebanon comes from its different communities—it has always been a melting pot of people and cultures," she says. "So many people are leaving. If I go, another little bit of this country's culture will vanish with me," she says.

Instead, she hopes to use her jewelry brand, Inspiration of Beirut, to prompt conversations about Lebanon's diverse cultural heritage, drawing on her knowledge of the country's past to remind people of a time when different communities coexisted more harmoniously. Looking past the divisions that have splintered society since the outbreak of civil war in 1975, she describes the shared Lebanese passion for enjoying life and points to the county's 1960s heyday, when Beirut, with its glamorous hotels, restaurants, and beach clubs, was known as the Paris of the Middle East. "In Lebanon, we love to have fun. It's a way of living. Even if a woman is poor, she tries to dress well and wear jewelry. It's part of our culture," she says.

As conflict looms and the Lebanese wait to see whether their country will be dragged into another war, Abukhater worries that the last vestiges of this era will vanish forever. "We are fighting to keep cultural liberty and freedom of expression. If the war happens, many will leave, and the fanatics will take over," she says.

Already, the impacts are being felt, and she has noticed a slump in sales. "No one is in the mood to buy anything. They are waiting to see if the war will happen," she says.

Abukhater's pieces use gold and silver, with prices starting at around $160 for a pair of gold earrings. All are handmade by Lebanese artisans, passing from the artist who draws up her designs to a jewelry maker who crafts the structure, a specialist to add the enamel, and another person to polish each piece. In the future, she hopes to open her own atelier and employ many of these artisans in-house. But that will depend on the situation in Lebanon, which is reeling from multiple crises, even without the specter of war.

Some days, life feels too hard, and Abukhater is tempted to join the exodus from her country. On those days, she tells herself that when her daughter finishes school, they will move abroad and start afresh. "But then I think, who will stay? Some people must stay and fight for our way of living." So she is channeling her energies into Inspiration of Beirut to remind people of a time when Lebanese from all communities celebrated their shared identity.

With an Innovation Hub grant from Ideas Beyond Borders, she is opening an online store accompanied by a social media campaign to advertise her products. She also plans to stage a pop-up stall in the mall, where she can engage with customers and tell them the story behind her brand. "I tell people it draws on a time when there was no war, when Lebanon was calm, and people came from all over the world to enjoy our way of life—to go from the beach to the mountains in an hour, enjoy good Mediterranean food and soak up the sunshine.

IDEAS BEYOND BORDERS

INNOVATION HUB

Tripoli by bike

A courier company challenged the dominance of cars in Lebanon's second city

Bicycles are becoming a more common sight in the streets of Tripoli. Image: Natheer Halawani

Nour Lachin doesn't wear a helmet when she cycles around Tripoli. The idea makes her laugh. The city in North Lebanon is not easy to navigate by bike—roads are choked with traffic, cars park on pavements, and motorbikes accelerate through the gaps with little regard for rules. But that hasn't stopped Lachin from riding her bike through the streets, even before it became fashionable in recent years as more residents discover an alternative way to travel around Lebanon's busy second city.

"I love cycling, when I'm on my bike I feel free," says the 28-year-old, who jumped at the opportunity to work with Wasil, a courier company that pioneered the two-wheeled trend in Tripoli. "I was very excited when a friend told me the delivery was done by bikes," says Lachin.

In the past, it was unusual to see women cycling in Tripoli, which is traditionally viewed as more conservative than the Lebanese capital, Beirut. But in recent years, female cyclists have become regular road users, challenging patriarchal norms and claiming their right to travel by bike. "The new generation is more daring and willing to demand equality," says Lachin.

There's also an element of necessity driving the shift to cycling in Tripoli, which was already Lebanon's poorest city, even before the pandemic and economic crisis pushed thousands more people below the poverty line. "I always wanted a bike and to stand up for my rights, but the biggest motive for me now is that cycling is much cheaper than taxis," adds Lachin.

LEBANON

Natheer Halawani (back left) is an active campaigner for cycling in Tripoli. Image: Natheer Halawani

For those without a car, there are few alternatives in Tripoli, where public transport is extremely limited. Wasil founder Natheer Halawani has always traveled by bike and made it his mission to encourage others to do the same, becoming the bicycle mayor of Tripoli in 2018 to raise awareness about the advantages of cycling. "It helps me exercise every day, makes my commute more enjoyable, and minimizes my carbon footprint. Plus, the speed at which you cycle is the perfect pace to enjoy and explore the city," says the 36-year-old.

Halawani started cycling when he was 15 and had limited funds to take taxis. "I decided a bike would be a better investment," he says. During the pandemic, he bumped into a friend, another cyclist, who was delivering food to someone in need. "In the lockdown, Lebanese were only allowed to travel by bicycle—walking or traveling by car were banned. I had the idea for Wasil right away," he says.

At first, it was just a bit of fun to occupy the extra hours during lockdown evenings. "We picked a name, made a logo, and scoped out interest. People loved it," he says. Then, he secured a grant for $1,000 to purchase some bikes, followed by more grants for larger sums, including an Innovation Hub grant from Ideas Beyond Borders. "We covered Beirut and Tripoli with ten members of staff, including seven delivery riders," he adds.

All Wasil deliveries were done by bike, focusing mainly on non-perishable items like clothing and accessories. In time, Halawani hopes to improve the environment for bicycles, collaborating with NGOs to install bike racks on buses and host events that encourage more people to take up cycling. To date, Wasil has carried out close to 1,800 deliveries, amounting to around 16,000km traveled by bike instead of a car. "That's a lot of carbon emissions saved," Halawani adds.

Cars are still the primary mode of transport in Tripoli, where gridlocked streets and the furious honk of car horns are part of everyday life. At present, there are only two bike lanes covering very small sections of the city and no safe storage options for people who want to park their bikes outside. But gradually, cyclists are becoming ubiquitous in the city's streets, which reassures Halawani that progress might be possible.

"I used to look out of my window and see a few bikes an hour; now there's one a minute," says Halawani. "And the biggest change, what's really beautiful, is that it's mostly women riding them."

The war in Gaza has impacted many small businesses in Lebanon. Sadly, Natheer Halawani was forced to close Wasil in early 2024 after several investors pulled out due to the deteriorating security situation. He plans to channel the experience he gained into future projects.

Family fortunes: the extraordinary story of Halabi Bookshop

A combination of business acumen and stubborn determination drove Lana Halabi to salvage a shuttered family bookshop and transform it into a cultural institution

Abdullah Halabi transformed the family business into a bookshop in the nineties. Image: Natheer Halawani

It will be difficult for the Halabi family to leave the building on Jalloul Street in Kaskas Beirut. It was here, in 1958, that Hussein Halabi started a small grocery store that would survive war, economic crises, and political turmoil to become one of Lebanon's leading bookshops. These days, the name is well-known on Lebanon's cultural scene, but for a long time, the tiny store was inaccessible, its entrance blocked by the sheer volume of unsold books packed into a 27-square-meter space.

This is what confronted Hussein Halabi's granddaughter Lana Halabi when she decided to re-launch the shop in 2016. In an age where independent bookstores struggle against internet giants, friends and colleagues said it was foolhardy to invest in a neighborhood book business. But nine years after quitting her job to revive Halabi Bookshop, Lana has proved the naysayers wrong. Now, the Halabi name is widely known. "We get a lot of messages from the Lebanese diaspora saying how proud they feel. It's really heart-warming," she says.

The journey has been turbulent, even for Lebanon, where the past five years have brought financial collapse, pandemic lockdowns, the Beirut port blast,

◉ LEBANON

Halabi Bookshop after the entrance became inaccessible.

political crisis, and the war in Gaza. That's before factoring in the emotional baggage that comes with taking over a family business. "If I had decided to start a bookshop from scratch, it would have been 50 percent less hassle," Lana says. Yet Halabi has thrived, becoming a community hub and cultural icon that harnesses the power of the written word to bring people from across the country together in difficult times.

Now, the business is growing and needs more space. A grant from Ideas Beyond Borders has helped make this happen, funding a new warehouse to support the bookshop operations, store their stock, and fulfill orders for their upcoming E-commerce website.

For Lana, it's the culmination of a decade's work. "I have been dreaming about this growth for so long, and now it's here," she says. Looking around the little shop, where books are stacked on every surface, and shoppers settle down to read in pools of lamplight, it feels like home. But Lana has always been business-minded, which is why she was able to salvage the bookshop in a climate that has forced many other businesses to close. So, she will relinquish the old site, with its cherished memories and family history, and find a new premises to accommodate the evolving vision for Halabi Bookshop, with a coffee shop and bakery on-site, space for families with children, and opportunities to host larger cultural events.

Learning to love books

Abdullah Halabi wasn't always a reader. As a young man, he traveled frequently, ferrying currency between London and Washington for a Jordanian bank in the 1980s. Exploring these foreign cities, Abdullah browsed the bookshops and noticed people reading on the metro and at bus stops in the street. His boss at the bank had a large private library and would often ask him to source books. Inspired, he began to read more. When his father Hussein Halabi fell sick, he returned to take over the family grocery store in Beirut and decided to turn it into a bookshop.

It was 1991, and the civil war that raged in Lebanon from 1975 had just ended. People were starting to spend money on books again. So, Abdullah reduced his grocery orders and started getting more books, buying up collections, and sourcing works on request from buyers. By then, he was reading widely—histories of Lebanon, biographies, and novels. "As a guardian of books, you have to read a lot of topics so you can help people choose what book is best for them." It's a role he now shares with his daughter Lana since she took over the family business in 2014.

A lot of Lana's time is now spent curating their collection, catering to different trends and tastes. Halabi Bookshop releases recommendations, which Lana compiles, researching the best books according to certain themes. The latest is parenting advice. "Parents need guidance, and this is the role of bookshops, to curate books. A lot of people trust us to start their reading journey," she says.

A cultural community

When she's not at the bookshop, or representing it at events, Lana takes her daughter to the park up the street. Horsh Beirut is the largest green space in the city, a verdant pocket of tree-lined pathways and grassy hillsides in the heart of a busy capital. "They call it the lung of Beirut. It's beautiful," she says.

Horsh Beirut used to be larger, spilling into the streets of Kaskas, which were once lined with trees. Back then, the area was a hub for creatives in the city, attracting actors, artists, and writers alongside visitors from across the Arab world. Among them were the director and writer Mohamed Salman, journalist Riad Taha and Hassan Alaa Eddin, the Lebanese actor and singer known as Shoushou, who lived in the same building as the Halabi family. "A lot of prominent people made this neighborhood their home," Abdullah says.

A lot has changed in Kaskas since those days. Over the years, demographics shifted, and the calm, leafy streets became noisy and crowded. Fewer people came to Kaskas, and the artistic ambiance drifted away. But Halabi Bookshop has given them a reason to come back, drawing creatives, intellectuals, and everyday readers from across the country to participate in the renaissance of this cultural gem.

"We still have people from all over Lebanon visiting Halabi because we re-created that kind of atmosphere," Lana says. "People of different backgrounds tell me they are proud to break those barriers and come to an area they wouldn't normally visit." It is one of the many unexpected rewards of reviving the bookshop, which has proved to be much more than a local business. "We are serving the country as a whole, not just the neighborhood. And the international community too—it's even become a tourist attraction," she says.

Honoring the collection

This makes the prospect of moving easier, because it's a role they will carry with them to the new Halabi Bookshop site. During difficult times, like the COVID-19 lockdowns, when the shop was forced to close, or the currency crash, which destroyed many small businesses across Lebanon, messages of support from the wider community kept Lana going. "People who have never been to Lebanon write and say they hope to come and visit Halabi. There are many beautiful messages," she says.

Many of the messages are on social media, where Halabi has an active network. This is where Lana took the first tentative steps to transform the business in 2014, building a following to support her plans, which initially focused on organizing and selling her father's huge collection. Over time, it had grown to around 100,000 books and magazines, but even when he ran out of space, Abdullah Halabi carried on collecting. "He would buy them from people who moved abroad, or from the children of old people who passed away," Lana says.

The collection included old and rare books covering a huge span of subjects in Arabic, English, French, Russian, Dutch, German, and Italian. There were magazines too, stretching back more

◉ LEBANON

than half a century—old copies of The Economist, National Geographic, and Newsweek, among others, chronicling global affairs across the decades. Several times he offered the books to libraries of NGOs, but there was never a reply. "At times, I was willing to give away all the books, but no one wanted to invest in a social, cultural project," he says.

As floor space disappeared under piles of books, he stored new purchases at home, cramming them into every corner and stacking them on surfaces, to the frustration of his wife. Some ended up on the roof, where they got damaged. Others were kept in a rented site and later stolen. As the new millennium dawned, sales dwindled and the bookshop became harder and harder to access. No one knew what to do with the small space that heaved with books.

So, the collection stayed in the small shop and the family home, gathering dust and provoking Lana's mother, who would berate Abdullah for spending so much on books. "She got frustrated, my mother. During the years he was collecting books, they weren't profitable at all, and our financial status was declining." By the time Lana decided to revive the business, the shop had been inaccessible for 15 years. "It started as a personal thing—I wanted my father to know that all the things he had collected were of value."

She also wanted to create a new source of income for her parents so they could enjoy a better lifestyle as they grew older. Lana had built a successful career in fashion and retail. If she could sell clothes and shoes, surely she could sell books too? She began by building a presence online to engage people with Halabi's journey. Weekends were spent at street fairs and any event where she could sell stock, collaborating with similar initiatives in Lebanon to build their network. Gradually, she carved out space for Halabi Bookshop on the cultural scene.

Her life at that time was a blur, but she knew how important it was to familiarize people with the Halabi name. The 59th edition of the Beirut Arab International Book Fair—the oldest book fair in the Arab world—was due to begin in November

Halabi Bookshop today.
Image: Natheer Halawani.

They still had a big fridge from the days when it was a grocery, but even that was stuffed with newspapers and magazines. The task seemed monumental.

"There was this big mental obstacle towards re-opening the shop," she says. Lana's brother agreed to put up some money, but it was a while before her family understood her vision for the tattered little store or shared her faith in its future.

Lebanon has long been a hub for publishing in the Middle East, helped by comparatively relaxed censorship rules, a prolific creative community, and superior printing facilities. Ahead of other Arab countries in tolerating free speech, it was known as the Switzerland of the Middle East, a place for Arabic authors and poets to publish their work. By the time Lana took over, the scene had changed, and two or three big book chains dominated the sector—the rest were small businesses like Halabi run by book collectors, and many were struggling to survive.

In 2017, their first fully operational year, several prominent old bookshops in Lebanon closed. Yet elsewhere, independent bookstores were re-emerging. "I read this article about how indie bookshops started coming back to life after 2015 in the US and UK. It was because neighborhoods needed community spaces," Lana says. This was the vision she set about realizing—a community space that felt warm and inviting, somewhere safe and welcoming for people to read and discuss their favorite works. She chose a deep red shade for the woodwork and placed colorful rugs on the freshly polished floors. Then, after a six-month renovation project, she restocked the shelves.

Sales were strong from the start, so Lana reinvested the proceeds to diversify their stock. "I was bad at managing the cash flow, then I gradually learnt," she says.

In 2017 they began to host events, including a traveling book club and storytelling sessions for children. Soon, Lana found herself crossing the country, hosting sessions in Tripoli, Saida, and the old Phoenician city of Sur. People would gather in public libraries, gardens, or sometimes a theater

2015 and all the serious players in the industry would be there. Lana was still working full-time and considered taking annual leave to attend the two-week fair. "That's when I thought, 'khalas' (enough), I need to quit my job for this mission."

A new bookshop

Four months later, Lana stood in front of the small shop that had sustained her family for so many years. The books had disappeared under the dust of several decades, and she wondered, briefly, whether to go ahead. As children, her mother used to take them all down to tidy the shop on Sundays.

◉ LEBANON

Lana Halabi. Image: Natheer Halawani

"Now there is war on the southern border and it's very stressful, we don't know how it could end. This is part of the resilience we grow as Lebanese — it's traumatizing in a way but also made us stronger. Given everything we have passed through, I know I can conquer anything."

Lana Halabi
Co-founder of Halabi Bookshop

space. "We used to collaborate with initiatives from civil society like ours that were having an impact," she says. Back in Beirut, the space in front of the bookshop became a regular spot for storytelling, tea parties, and other cultural gatherings. Neighbors would bring cakes, and passersby would stop to listen. "It was a very warm environment," Lana says.

News of their success rippled around the country as media outlets came to document the shop's makeover. Two years went by quickly as the Halabi enterprise continued to grow. Still, they struggled financially. "We got a lot of support from the media—people were emotionally invested. But it was very hard for us to get any financing from the entrepreneurial ecosystem in Lebanon; they saw us as a traditional business," she says. Then, the currency crisis hit in 2019, and six months later, the country went into lockdown as the COVID-19 pandemic spread around the world.

Staying afloat

As the streets fell silent and footfall slowed, Lana switched to survival mode. With the value of the Lebanese lira plummeting and protests gripping the country, sales dropped. "It was hard, all our accounts were collapsing, the devaluation really ruined everything, then came more difficulties like the Beirut blast." By then, the bookshop was supporting the whole family. "I didn't have the luxury to fail. I was responsible for my family, the pets, everything. I always had to find ways to go on and survive."

She used the lull to digitize their stock, which turned out to be one of the best things she has done for the bookshop. Still, taking these decisions as a solo entrepreneur has been hard, and at times lonely. During the currency crisis, when several staff members left, or when she fell pregnant and had to make sure everything could run without her, the hurdles felt insurmountable. "Now there is war on the southern border, and it's very stressful. We don't know how it could end. This is part of the resilience we develop as Lebanese—it's traumatizing in a way but also made us stronger," she says.

For Lana, success lies in accepting challenges. "Given everything we have passed through, I know I can conquer anything," she says.

A new chapter

By 2023, Halabi Bookshop was back to running events, and in January this year, they relaunched the book club. The new warehouse space is operational and Lana is busy planning the next phase of expansion. Finally, a decade after she embarked on the project, the family business is growing. These days, it really is a family enterprise. Her mother is the assistant manager and runs the shop while Lana and her brother visit book fairs, host cultural events, and attend speaking engagements abroad.

In recent years, Lana has been invited to speak at the Abu Dhabi International Book Fair, the Book Arsenal in Kyiv, and numerous events in Lebanon. Sharing her journey with others reminds her of what she has achieved and how far they have come. However, one opportunity always evaded her. For years, she struggled to secure funding to grow the business. "After the economy collapsed, the appetite for investment shifted, and funding for cultural projects dried up," she says.

So, last year, she compiled the reasons their grant applications were rejected and addressed them one by one. She registered the business as a formal entity named Ficus SARL and put the whole enterprise in her name to manage legal affairs. She also formalized their employment structure and tidied their financial reports. It paid off. Last year, she had two breakthroughs—a microfinance investment loan and an Innovation Hub grant from Ideas Beyond Borders.

This, for Lana, is what makes running Halabi Bookshop so rewarding. The entrepreneur is a problem solver, she says, and finding ways to make the business thrive is a powerful validation. "It's not about the money—there's a limit to what you can make in this industry." But the impact is limitless, and this is where her ambition leans. "The messages we get from our community are inspirational. They say we are bringing hope to Lebanon and that is what really drives me on."

📍 CRISIS RESPONSE

Crisis Response

Ideas Beyond Borders in times of crisis

The afternoon of February 6th, 2023 found Ideas Beyond Borders in an emergency meeting. In the early hours of that morning, a devastating earthquake had sent waves of destruction across southern Turkey and northern Syria and the world woke to scenes of horror flashing across their screens. Entire cities were flattened and millions of lives destroyed in the 7.8-magnitude earthquake, which struck near Gaziantep as people slept. More devastation followed amid a series of aftershocks, including a 7.5-magnitude quake that afternoon.

As the team gathered, reports of the thousands killed were climbing minute by minute, and a desperate search to pull people from the rubble was underway. Turkey is better equipped to handle emergencies than most of the countries IBB operates in, and countries around the world were already preparing to send supplies. At Ideas Beyond Borders, our mandate focuses on long-term development rather than crisis response, but there are times when our network and expertise can provide invaluable support during an emergency.

Gathering together that afternoon, we considered where that assistance was needed and prepared a list of people who could help. Before the earthquake, this part of southern Turkey was home to 1.7 million refugees who fled the war in neighboring Syria. Many were now destitute, without shelter, food, water, and other essential supplies. "Pictures showing the scale of destruction were rolling in, and we could see that the death toll would continue to rise. We wanted to help those with nowhere else to go," says Faisal Al Mutar, President of Ideas Beyond Borders.

INNOVATION HUB

Hani Hammadeh delivering aid packages funded by Ideas Beyond Borders to Syrians after the earthquake

CRISIS RESPONSE

Earthquake relief in Syria

Over a year later, the wounds are still raw across affected provinces and many are in temporary accommodation. Over 55,000 people were killed, and more than 850,000 buildings collapsed as a result of the February 6 earthquakes, leaving hundreds of thousands dependent on aid.

Within days, a massive international response was underway as dozens of countries provided financial and logistical support, sending ships and planes with supplies to Turkey. But across the border in Syria, help was slower to arrive as the Assad regime obstructed humanitarian aid to rebel-held areas, wasting precious time as people searched for relatives under the rubble.

When Huthayfa Abduljabbar arrived in Aleppo with aid packages funded by Ideas Beyond Borders, he found groups of people huddled in tents with scraps of food, no hygiene facilities, and nothing to clean their wounds. "Their situation was dire… Hardly anyone was helping them," he recalls.

Ideas Beyond Borders funded a series of relief efforts in Syria to help plug the shortfall in aid, working with water filtration company LifeStraw to provide 789 filter systems so that people would have access to safe water, sending boxes of medical and healthcare supplies through multiple partners on the ground, and funding new job opportunities to give people the chance of a fresh start.

"One of our strengths is being nimble. Acting quickly at times like this is crucial, which is why we step in to help when our support can make a positive impact in emergency situations," says Al Mutar. Operating across multiple countries in diverse fields gives Ideas Beyond Borders access to a vast network of local actors who are often uniquely positioned to offer support. That's why we are able to respond quickly and in a targeted way, to address the unmet needs of survivors in the immediate aftermath of an emergency.

Rebuilding a school in Kabul

At Ideas Beyond Borders, we focus on educating and empowering people to create lasting change in their communities. We address the root cause of problems so that they cease to exist, hoping that one day, the need for our support also ends. But there are times when we can be on hand to help in a crisis, sending money quickly for a targeted emergency response.

Like in Kabul, when a suicide bomber blew up an education center, killing 53 students as they sat mock tests ahead of their university entrance exams. Within days of the attack on September 30, 2022, Ideas Beyond Borders released funds to rebuild the Dasht-e-Barchi branch of the Kaaj Education Institution as the community rallied to restore access to learning for their surviving classmates.

The institution's founder Mukhtar Modabber told us that rebuilding the center was the best way to offer support. "We cannot stop, if we do, these kids' futures will be destroyed, and we will have more violence and outrage in society. This is our way of pushing back against injustice and fighting towards a better future," he said. Weeks later, students were back in class, with additional security covered by IBB's grant.

Attacks like this are not infrequent in Afghanistan, where schools are often targeted by extremist groups, particularly in minority neighborhoods like Dasht-e-Barchi, which is home to the oppressed Hazara community. "Countless times this has happened in this area, but people here still want to fight and continue the struggle for their right to education," Modabber, 30, told us.

At other times, our response is part of a broader effort to provide access to knowledge and fight back against extremism. When protests broke out across Iran following the death of Kurdish woman Mahsa Amini in police custody, Iranian authorities launched a violent crackdown. The morality police arrested the 22-year-old for allegedly violating the country's strict dress codes for women and her death a few days later sparked a global outcry that played out for months on the streets of Iran.

Spotlight on the streets of Iran

To undermine demonstrations and silence reports of rights violations against protesters, the Iranian regime imposed sweeping internet blackouts and blocked access to platforms including WhatsApp and Instagram. Our response sought to counter this censorship by providing VPN access to a monitoring group inside Iran. Hengaw Organization for Human Rights gathered video and photographic evidence of the violations being perpetrated and shared them with sources outside Iran.

The VPN enabled Hengaw to provide "authentic news on the brutality of the regime" and "broadcast its true image to the world," Faraz Firouzi, the organization's legal advisor, said.

As solidarity protests massed in cities around the world, footage like this was vital to maintain public pressure on the Iranian regime. "The days when tyrannical regimes could act with impunity and deny their atrocities on the world stage ended with the advent of the internet and the spread of social media," says Al Mutar. "It's up to organizations like Ideas Beyond Borders to keep the channels of communication open and provide those fighting back with the tools they need to overcome oppression."

Some of the challenges we confront, like internet censorship, are recent and require a state-of-the-art response. Others, like natural disasters and suicide attacks, are sadly familiar. Ideas Beyond Borders aims to meet every crisis anew and respond to the unique demands of each situation. It's a philosophy that applies to all of our work across the Middle East, Iran, and Afghanistan, where people on the ground devise and implement the projects we support. We empower local actors to serve the communities they represent, bringing hope, opportunities, and solutions to complex challenges, whether it's crisis response or a long-term resolution that promises to change the future for the lives we touch.

CRISIS RESPONSE

VPNs bypass the internet blackout in Iran

As authorities clamped down on protests in Iran, the Hengaw Organization for Human Rights kept communications channels open

Ideas Beyond Borders provided VPN access to rights groups during internet blackouts in Iran. Photo: Shutterstock

When the internet went dark in Iran, Sepi Beigi started to panic. The last time this happened was in 2019, when an estimated 1,500 people were killed as Iranian authorities shot protesters at close range in what became known as Bloody November.

In September 2022, after widespread protests broke out across Iran, she feared the same thing was happening again. Unable to communicate with friends and family in the country, Beigi, who lives in London, was glued to her phone, desperate for updates but terrified of the news they might bring. "I can't do anything. I just share messages on social media to try and spread the message. I feel so helpless," she said at the time.

Anti-government demonstrations broke out on September 16 in Iran following the death of 22-year-old Mahsa Amini in police custody. Amini, who was from Iran's Kurdish minority, was visiting the country's capital, Tehran when she was hauled in for questioning by the country's notorious morality police for violating Iran's strict dress codes for women.

Her death three days later sparked widespread fury, particularly among women who were at the forefront of the protests, making headlines around the world as they burned their hijabs and cut their hair to symbolize their opposition to the regime.

The response was brutal. Activists reported that at least 19,200 people were detained and 537 were killed in a crackdown that included the execution of at least seven protesters. Alongside violent suppression, authorities also used internet blackouts to hinder communication between protesters, making it difficult to determine the actual number of casualties as Iranians outside the country waited desperately for news.

To counter the internet blackout and help volunteers document the rights violations being perpetrated inside Iran, Ideas Beyond Borders provided VPN access to the Hengaw Organization for Human Rights. The organization, which focuses on violations against Kurdish communities in Iran, worked with volunteers on the ground to share evidence of violence by Iranian security forces against protesters.

"These are the people providing video footage, photos, and reports of real-time events, so it's vital that they are able to share it with the outside world and prevent the regime from covering up their atrocities," said Hussein Ibrahim, Iraq country director at Ideas Beyond Borders.

Most of the IT infrastructure in Iran is controlled by the regime's security forces, allowing them to shut down public and private internet servers to conceal the violence being perpetrated on the streets. "The regime is cutting internet access to impede the free flow of information so that the world won't see their violence and oppression," said Faraz Firouzi, legal advisor of the Hengaw Organization for Human Rights. "By accessing this VPN, we will be able to provide authentic news on the brutality of the regime so that its true image will be broadcast to the world."

"It is vital to provide the world with this on-the-ground footage in order to prevent more massacres of Iranians by the regime while declaring to the world that Iranians are calling for a regime change and their claim is not limited to a change of hijab regulations," he added.

Around the world, demonstrators came together to share their support, with protests in countries including the UK, the US, France, Turkey, Greece, and Germany.

In London's Trafalgar Square, hundreds gathered to demand basic freedoms in Iran and an end to the regime's draconian dress laws for women. "They have shut down the internet in Iran, and people are fighting without anything, just their bare hands and the world should know, should support," said Shirin Naseri, speaking at a protest in London weeks after the protests broke out in Iran. "We do not want the compulsory hijab, we want freedom, we want women's revolution."

Others voiced concern over the internet blackout. "They cut out the internet, there's no social media working, no WhatsApp working, so they can't let people outside the country know what's happening in Iran. So that's what we're trying to do here, to let people know what's happening in Iran," said Mohammed, who withheld his last name.

> "By accessing this VPN, we will be able to provide authentic news on the brutality of the regime so that its true image will be broadcast to the world."
>
> **Faraz Firouzi**
> Legal advisor of the Hengaw Organization for Human Rights

Internet blackouts are part of a wider cyber surveillance system used by Iranian authorities to hinder mobilization efforts among protesters and hide police brutality from the outside world. Internet watchdog Netblocks described the latest shutdowns as "the most severe internet restrictions since the November 2019 massacre."

Steps taken by the US government to expand internet access in Iran included lifting sanctions restrictions on private companies offering uncensored internet access to Iranians. This allowed Elon Musk to activate his satellite broadband service Starlink inside Iran. With Ideas Beyond Borders support, Hengaw was then able to use the VPN access to share videos, photographs, and other content documenting events on the ground in Iran.

"What Iran has right now is a new generation that has no fear and is willing to face a great amount of danger, but unfortunately, the Iranian government has shown that internet blackouts come with the implicit threat of violence against peaceful protesters. We hope that our support will keep them safe and connected to us all concerned about their freedom and future," said Faisal Al Mutar, President of Ideas Beyond Borders.

CRISIS RESPONSE

'They have given up hope': Syrians after the earthquake

Turkey is home to around 3.7 million Syrian refugees who fled a brutal war to start their lives again. As they faced another catastrophe, IBB stepped in to help

Hundreds of thousands of homes were destroyed in Turkey and Syria

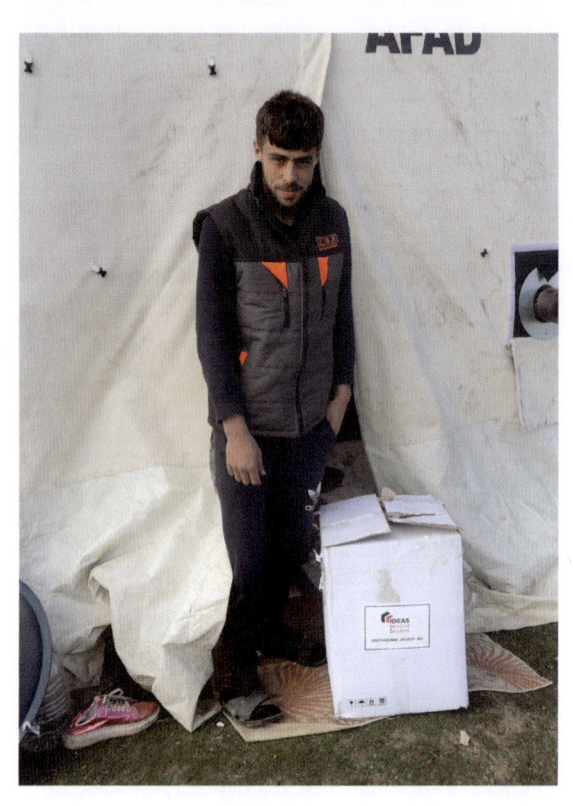

Over four million people relied on aid in northern Syria even before the earthquake struck

It wasn't pain that Hani Hammadeh saw as he delivered aid to Syrians in Turkey in February 2023. Nor desperation among families whose lives were destroyed by the double earthquakes that flattened towns and villages across southern Turkey and northern Syria, claiming over 55,000 lives. "I didn't see anything, not even gratitude," said Hammadeh. "There was no reaction; they were just numb."

Hammadeh secured funding from Ideas Beyond Borders to support Syrian victims of the 7.8-magnitude earthquake that struck near the Turkish city of Gaziantep on February 6, 2023, causing a wave of destruction that extended across an area of more than 500 kilometers. A second earthquake measuring 7.5 magnitude followed hours later, adding to the damage. As the scale of the catastrophe became clear, Ideas Beyond Borders allocated an emergency budget, partnering with our innovators in Turkey and Iraq to help Syrians whose refugee status limits their ability to access support or rebuild their lives.

"The earthquakes were a disaster for the whole country, but for Syrian refugees in Turkey, the impact is particularly acute," said Faisal Al Mutar, President of Ideas Beyond Borders. "After surviving a brutal war, migration, and now a natural disaster, they are back in the rubble, faced with the daunting task of starting again once more."

Uncertain future

Before the earthquakes, many Syrians in Turkey lived day to day, surviving on odd jobs. In the aftermath of the disaster, many had no means of earning a living, with local economies at a standstill in towns and cities rendered uninhabitable. While Turkish survivors could seek work in the country's northern provinces, Syrian refugees had to remain where they were registered or risk deportation.

Majd Albasha is another Innovation Hub grantee who offered support to the Syrian community. After surviving a perilous crossing to escape the war at home, he built a new life in Turkey, founding a business and providing employment to other Syrian refugees in Istanbul. With IBB support, he created two new vacancies at his company to provide opportunities for Syrians who lost their livelihoods in the earthquake.

"The way I see it, this is two families that will be given another chance at rebuilding their lives here. They are living through a nightmare, so we will focus on providing them with psychosocial support as well as help them find a home, furniture and other necessities," he said.

His family was asleep at their home in Istanbul when the earthquake hit. "We woke up and heard the news. It was an awful thing to see." They ran around the house gathering clothes and household items, whatever they could donate. Weeks later, he was still in shock. "For ages I couldn't let my daughter sleep in her room in case something happened and I needed to act fast," he said.

Lack of opportunities

Even before the earthquake, life was difficult for Syrians in Turkey, where many lack work permits and live below the poverty line. Turkey hosts the world's largest number of Syrian refugees—around 3.6 million—but attitudes have hardened as the war in Syria drags on, and many are unable to return. Instead, they endure second-class status in a country that increasingly resents their presence.

"We have every kind of challenge from racism and discrimination to lack of work and limited freedom of movement around the country," says Albasha, who has heard multiple accounts of abusive language targeting Syrians accessing aid. "Now it's even worse. There is nothing for them. The situation is so bad," he says.

IBB's grant paid the salaries of two new employees at Albasha's digital marketing company, Apollo Agency, for six months and covered their social security. "It gives them access to enter the job market here, which is incredibly competitive, so it's a good push for them to build better lives in Turkey," he said.

For many, the earthquakes made this an impossible dream. Weeks later, families were sleeping in tents, train carriages, and the ruins of mosque courtyards, with little thought beyond immediate survival as they surveyed the wreckage of lives that had already been rebuilt, often multiple times. In desperation, tens of thousands of Syrians returned to rebel-held northern Syria, where the situation remains volatile, and around 4.1 million people relied on aid even before the earthquake struck. But the situation they faced there was even worse.

Hani Hammadeh delivering aid packages funded by Ideas Beyond Borders to Syrians after the earthquake

📍 CRISIS RESPONSE

Syrian graphic designer Şahd Kazar found employment after the earthquake with Majd Albasha's marketing company Apollo Agency

The outlook in Syria

Despite mounting pressure from the international community, efforts to get aid to help survivors in Syria, where an estimated 6,000 people were killed in the earthquake, faltered in the face of political wrangling with the Assad regime. According to Amnesty International, the Syrian government and Turkey-backed opposition groups blocked at least 100 trucks carrying food, medical supplies, and tents from reaching Kurdish-majority neighborhoods in Aleppo between February 9 and February 22, when the need for emergency support was most critical.

Huthayfa Abduljabbar worked hard to get basic necessities across the border from Iraq to support survivors in Aleppo, where the ravages of war are hard to distinguish from the destruction caused by the earthquake.

Often, whole families were buried under multistorey buildings, with just a few survivors pulled from the rubble. "There were many people living in small tents with a kid from one family, the adults from another, and more children from third and fourth families. It was like a puzzle," Abduljabbar said.

The food boxes he distributed contained detergents, first aid kits, and food, and other necessities to support up to 300 families. "Their situation was dire, with little food, no hygiene, and nothing to clean their wounds. Hardly anyone was helping them," he recalls.

Politics over people

The UN was widely criticized for waiting to secure Syrian government permission before sending international aid to opposition areas, leaving families to dig their relatives out of the rubble.

"The earthquakes have pushed tens of thousands of people in Aleppo who were already struggling due to a decade-long armed conflict into further deprivation. Yet even in this moment of desperation, the Syrian government and armed opposition groups have pandered to political considerations

Water filtration systems from LifeStraw provided vital access to clean water

and taken advantage of people's misery to advance their own agendas," Aya Majzoub, Amnesty International's Deputy Director for the Middle East and North Africa said at the time.

One of the most immediate needs was access to clean water, so Ideas Beyond Borders partnered with LifeStraw, a water filtration company that supplies systems designed for low-resource and humanitarian settings, to provide almost 800 systems for earthquake survivors in Syria. There is a huge need, and that's going to remain the case for a while because so much infrastructure has been destroyed," said Tara MacDowell, senior manager of social impact at LifeStraw.

Long road to recovery

A month after the earthquakes, rescue workers stopped pulling bodies from the debris and handed the sites over to excavators who began clearing the rubble. Focus shifted to the future amid projections for rebuilding towns and cities across Syria and Turkey. Estimates ran to the tens of billions, and over a year later, the real work had only just begun. But for those whose lives were upended in the tragedy, recovery is more than a matter of money.

"The Syrians worked hard to rebuild their lives in Turkey. Most of them work long hours to buy just enough food to survive. Now their lives have been destroyed again, and many have given up hope," Hani Hammadeh said. "I've seen this in humans. After long exposure to tragedy, they start to feel nothing—they aren't sad or angry or hungry. Nothing shows on their faces."

Many felt frightened and abandoned but what worried Hammadeh the most were those who barely spoke. In a crisis of such magnitude, with hundreds of thousands displaced, they knew there was little point in pressing their case. "There are many reasons why refugees aren't getting the help they need. Syrians are nobody's priority," he added.

◉ CRISIS RESPONSE

'Every Afghan is angry': Protesters unite following school blast

After dozens of students were killed in a suicide attack on the Kaaj Education Institution the community defended their right to learn

The attack on Kaaj Education Institution occurred as students sat mock tests ahead of their university entrance exams. Image: Paeez Jahanbin

It was Friday, a weekend day in Afghanistan, when the founder of Kaaj Education Institution received the call. A suicide bomber had attacked a class full of students at the Dasht-e-Barchi branch in Kabul—dozens were dead. Reaching the scene, Mukhtar Modabber realized the extent of the damage. "I saw a lot of dead people. One was my sister. We tried to move the bodies, but there were no ambulances. We did it all by ourselves."

There were 53 killed and over 100 injured in the attack on September 30 2022, which targeted students as they sat mock tests in preparation for their university entrance exams. The attack was later claimed by the Khorasan arm of ISIS in Afghanistan.

It's not the first time the school, a private education facility with branches across the country, has been attacked by militants. This branch, located in a predominantly Shiite Muslim neighborhood, was attended by students from the minority Hazara population, who have been subject to a series of devastating attacks over recent years.

In 2018, there were over 100 casualties following an attack on the school, which subsequently moved to a new location, rebranding and investing in more security before reopening its doors. This time, they decided to stay and rebuild the shattered classrooms so students could continue to study in their community. "Countless times this has happened in this area, but people here still want to fight and continue the struggle for their right to education," Modabber, 30, says.

The damage was substantial, with windows shattered, ceilings destroyed, doors blown out, and chairs melted by the blast. But the students and their families, including some of those whose children died in the blast, were outside the school on Saturday morning, offering to help rebuild and clean up the mess. "They want to continue studying and

The community rallied round to help re-build Kaaj Education Institution with funding from Ideas Beyond Borders. Image: Paeez Jahanbin

we promised that we are going to do everything we can to rebuild and start again," Modabber said at the time.

Ideas Beyond Borders provided a grant to cover the cost of restoring the school and hiring extra security to protect students as they returned to class. While people in the community felt afraid, they were more horrified by the prospect of letting militant groups deny their children the opportunity to learn. "We cannot stop. If we do, these kids' futures will be destroyed, and we will have more violence and outrage in society," Modabber said. "This is our way of pushing back against injustice and fighting towards a better future."

By Sunday, demonstrations against the attack had spread to several provinces across Afghanistan, with young women turning out to defend their right to education under the Taliban, who banned girls from attending school after sixth grade. Most of those killed in the blast were young women aged between 18 and 24.

Reports of Taliban violence towards protesters fueled anger as people from different communities came together to express their outrage. "All ethnicities have joined together with the Hazaras in these protests because this attack was inhumane—the people killed were just kids, not politicians, not soldiers, just kids," said Modabber. "People are extremely tired (of the violence)…every Afghan is angry over this."

> *"Countless times this has happened in this area, but people here still want to fight and continue the struggle for their right to education (…). They want to continue studying and we promised that we are going to do everything we can to rebuild and start again."*

Mukhtar Modabber
Founder of the Kaaj
Education Institution

CRISIS RESPONSE

The tech team fighting misinformation in Arabic

Tech 4 Peace tackles the flood of false narratives circulating on Arabic social media, from ISIS propaganda and COVID-19 misinformation to state-sponsored disinformation

The clue could be something tiny, like the mobile phone number in an advert or the sign outside a shop. It's relatively easy to spot whether a photo is fake; you just have to know where to look, says Bahar Jasim, spokesperson at Tech 4 Peace. His team of 265 digital investigators spend hours every week scouring images, videos, and text to determine their origin. "It's relatively easy to track photos and videos; it just takes time," says Jasim.

Originally set up to counter ISIS propaganda in 2016, Tech 4 Peace has expanded to tackle disinformation in Arabic around other topics, including COVID-19 and the war in Ukraine. "There has been a lot of fake news here about Russia and Ukraine…I never expected to see our nation so divided by a war in the Western world," says Jasim.

But the interest is keenly felt in Iraq, where fake videos showing Russian troop landings or aircraft over Kyiv went viral, and conspiracy theories about the allegiances of Russian President Vladimir Putin and US President Joe Biden gained a lot of traction at the start of the war. "Iraqis like to follow global trends and analyze what's happening," he says. "Some people just share whatever comes onto their timeline without thinking, but others know it's fake news and do it deliberately to support their interests or cause harm," Jasim says.

While photos and videos offer a wealth of visual information and metadata that makes them easier to trace, text is more difficult. It can take days of sifting through documents and fact-checking sources to establish the veracity of a written rumor, and Tech 4 Peace staff work on a voluntary basis. "We all have day jobs. People do this in their spare time because they want to serve society and use their skills to give back."

It's also dangerous. Only Jasim's name is public because he resides in Europe—the rest of the team operates in secret out of Iraq. "We receive a lot of threats due to the sensitive nature of the cases we debunk," says Jasim.

He recalls the tragic fate of a man who was accused of being homosexual on social media because he had long, fair hair. The comments were widely shared, and a few weeks later, he was found dead in a rubbish container in Baghdad. "After that, we published an article asking people to stop pressing that share button without thinking," Jasim says.

In some cases, Tech 4 Peace can debunk false narratives and prevent further harm. After the battle to expel ISIS from Mosul, Iraq's rumor mill went into overdrive as authorities tried to root out sleeper cells. Tech 4 Peace received a desperate call from a man whose brother was arrested after his photo was captioned with the name of an ISIS fighter and circulated online. The person behind the image had fallen out with the victim weeks earlier and took revenge. In Iraq, acts like this can cost someone their life.

Tech 4 Peace was able to prove that the ISIS fighter in the picture had been dead for some time, and the findings were used to secure the innocent man's freedom. But the daily flood of false narratives is sometimes too much for the team to manage. "Our aim is to tackle every piece of fake news we find, but we do have to give priority if there is a type of false news that causes harm," Jasim says.

During the pandemic, Tech 4 Peace expanded to process the surge in fake advice and conspiracy theories flooding Iraqi social media. "It was a huge increase in our workload," Jasim recalls, pointing to the need to investigate medical advice, follow up with scientists, and verify case studies. Sometimes it was harmless, but much of the advice was dangerous, like the well-known television presenter who told audiences that alcohol could protect drinkers against COVID-19.

And the flood of false narratives has only increased since the height of the pandemic, which is why Ideas Beyond Borders gave Tech 4 Peace an Innovation Hub grant to offset the costs of staff members giving up their free time.

"These people act at great personal risk to debunk dangerous rumors and expose lies that contribute to the instability and hate underlying many of the problems facing Iraq," says Faisal Al Mutar, President of Ideas Beyond Borders. "Unfortunately, conspiracy theories and misinformation in Iraq are mainstream, so it's vital work at a time when it's becoming increasingly difficult to distinguish fact from fiction, not just in Iraq but across the world."

For Jasim, the aim is to make Tech 4 Peace universal by teaching people to verify information themselves. The organization offers free online courses in fact-checking and online security and they include details for each investigation at the bottom of the page so viewers can see exactly how it's done and what tools were used. "We want everyone in Iraq to be part of Tech 4 Peace so people can take charge, call out fake news and fight it by themselves," he says.

A Tech 4 Peace alert on misleading footage in a report by an Iraqi news channel about Russian fighter jets entering Ukrainian airspace in 2022

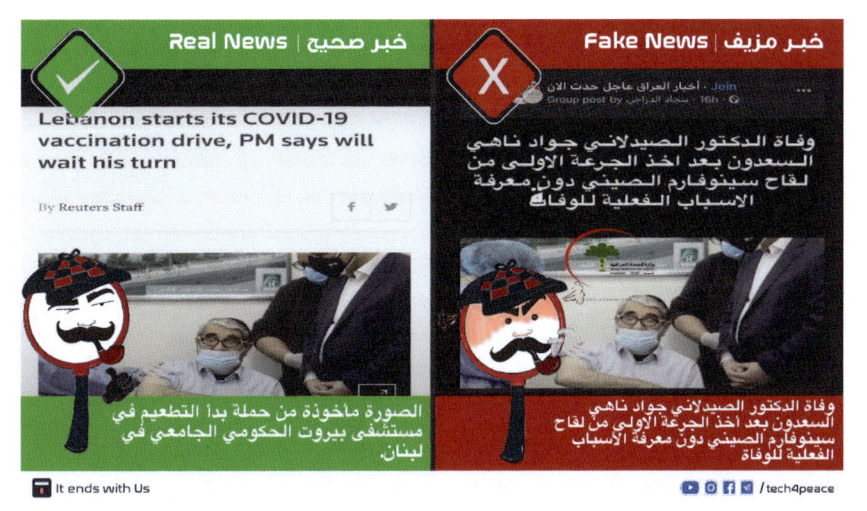

A Tech 4 Peace investigation refuted claims in this post that a pharmacist died after receiving the Covid-19 vaccination

CRISIS RESPONSE

Safety net for Kurds fleeing Iran

Amid killings, disappearances, and executions, some protesters were forced to leave Iran at a moment's notice

Gulbakh Bahrami is quick to recognize the suffering on the faces of Iranian Kurds. She knows what they have endured to reach Iraqi Kurdistan and the desperate state in which they arrive. "Most come through the mountains via smugglers, with only the clothes on their backs. They bring nothing with them, so they need everything—food, clothes, medical checkups, a place to live," says Bahrami, who founded the Hiway Rojhalat Organization to support Kurdish families fleeing Iran.

She remembers how it felt to reach safety after a long and dangerous journey, only to realize there is no plan for what comes next. "The hardest part is starting a new life from scratch; it's very difficult," she says. Bahrami and her husband fled Iran in 2010 after being arrested multiple times for their work as writers and activists. "The last time we were released on bail, we escaped, and then the news came that a prison sentence had been issued for us, so now we can never go back," she says.

IDEAS BEYOND BORDERS

INNOVATION HUB

Illustration by Lana Al-Jaf

Their journey to Iraqi Kurdistan was a grueling 16-hour slog on foot, with fear of arrest stalking every step. "There's a big chance you could get caught at any time, and we were worried about our four-year-old son—what would happen to him if they took us," she says. The family finally crossed the border into Iraqi Kurdistan, but in many ways, the hardest part was still to come. "It was very tough in the beginning. We worked every day from 6 am to midnight to make a life here."

The demonstrations across Iran following the death of 22-year-old Kurdish woman Mahsa Amini in police custody sparked another exodus of people, many fleeing violent repression from the regime. "They are mainly activists who were advocating for the rights of their nation and now they are under surveillance," Bahrami says. Most are just beginning the process of starting their lives in Iraqi Kurdistan, unsure how to find work, afford food, or secure a place to live. "If these people had stayed in Iran, they would probably have faced long-term prison sentences or execution," adds Bahrami.

At least 537 protesters were killed in the unrest, while another 19,200 were arrested, activists said, as the regime faced down the threat to its decades-long rule. Many of the Kurds Bahrami works with fled quickly as the danger grew. "When I provide help to these people it reminds me of the journey I took to get here. I feel I am helping myself because I was in their position years ago."

In the past six years, Bahrami estimates she has reached around 2,000 people, targeting 200 to 400 with each new project. An Innovation Hub grant from Ideas Beyond Borders is funding another round of support, allowing Bahrami to purchase food, clothing, school materials and medical supplies for people who suddenly find themselves with nothing, after becoming a target of the regime.

"These people have sacrificed everything for the future of their country and the belief that a better future is possible for Iran. Now they find themselves without a home, forced to leave behind all they know and start again," says Faisal Al Mutar, President of Ideas Beyond Borders. "The Hiway Rojhalat Organization is providing them with the means to do that, offering support and supplies when they need it most."

Bahrami knows she can never return to Iran, at least not under the current regime, but she's hopeful that a turning point is in sight. "This has been a long-awaited revolution. The regime has ruled the country for decades and oppressed its people, but the killing of Jina (Mahsa) Amini has triggered a new wave of fury. People are braver and bolder, not scared as they have been in the past. Maybe this time it will spread, and we will get our freedom."

IRAQ

"When I first had the idea, people actually opposed it and said it would be impossible, but now they are starting to see the change."

Kamiran Khalaf
Founder of Orshina Library in Sinjar

IDEAS BEYOND BORDERS

Author's note

I first heard about Ideas Beyond Borders in 2019. Faisal Al Mutar was giving a talk in London, and I was intrigued. What struck me was the ambition of his mission—to counter a region-wide culture of censorship with a team of student translators, often working in secret under restrictive regimes. Many were based in Mosul and had lived through the horrors of the ISIS occupation. They had seen their dreams extinguished as universities were shuttered and libraries burned to the ground. Working for IBB's House of Wisdom 2.0 translation program was a way to dispel the darkness and reclaim their city by forging new avenues to learning online.

The task was a huge undertaking. At that time, just three percent of internet content was available in Arabic, despite being the fourth most common language among users online. With MENA countries dominating the top 10 percent of media-oppressed countries, the vacuum felt terrifying. I had seen the effects of radicalization while working as a journalist in Jordan and Lebanon, speaking with desperate parents about the shadowy recruiters targeting their children on social media sites. IBB wanted to reach youth early, arming them with the knowledge to counter extremist material and challenge the radical ideologies being harnessed to manipulate minds.

Already, they had added more than 2.1 million words to Arabic Wikipedia with articles on evolution, religious diversity, female scientists, civil rights, philosophy, and literature—fields they felt were under-represented in Arabic online. I spoke with Ameen Al-Jaleeli, the university professor leading translation efforts in Mosul, who downloaded hundreds of Wikipedia articles before ISIS cut the internet in July 2016. Reading was the solace that sustained him as airstrikes pounded the city, proof that knowledge was limitless, even under an extremist regime.

When Mosul emerged from the conflict, blinking and battle-scarred in the summer of 2017, he vowed to strengthen his city against future attacks. IBB had a plan to reclaim the space militants had stolen. Beginning with Wikipedia, they would democratize access to information in environments where ruling regimes restrict the conversation and extremists use violence to intimidate and control. Word spread, and interest in the fledgling project grew. When I spoke with Al-Jaleeli in 2019, IBB had more than a million Facebook followers and over 40,000 daily views.

Soon, they would have another challenge to contend with as a new theater of misinformation arose to consume minds and endanger lives. That was the second time I encountered Ideas Beyond Borders, during the early days of the pandemic, when confusion around COVID-19 left a dangerous vacuum for conspiracy theories to ferment and panic to unfold. By then, I was living in Abu Dhabi, covering the impact of the virus as it spread worldwide. IBB was making videos in Arabic, debunking myths, translating medical advice, and countering the barrage of misinformation circulating online.

I saw for a second time the enormous scope of this project, which by then had translated more than 11 million words from books and Wikipedia articles into Arabic, with a growing team of over 200 student translators across the Middle East and later Afghanistan. Amid the deafening noise of partisan news crowding the digital space, here was a voice of reason that offered Arabic speakers factual information. It was a glimmer of hope during those strangely uncertain times.

A year later, Faisal contacted me again, sounding excited. He had another plan to empower people across the region, this time through a micro-grant program called the Innovation Hub. The program would put money in the hands of people with bold ideas, tackling the region's challenges one town or village at a time. Would I write the stories of these people and the impact they aimed to achieve?

Speaking with the first Innovation Hub grantees, it was clear that these were not the individuals who usually receive development funding. They were ordinary people without access to influential networks who saw a way to make things better, and IBB was giving them that scope. People like Zahraa Raad Abathar, who is teaching children about stranger danger, defying taboos to tackle important subjects that are sidelined in Iraq. Or Farhan Ibraheem, who is running freedom of expression workshops to protect young Yazidis speaking out about human rights violations in Sinjar. And many others, who are busy creating employment opportunities, upskilling communities, and providing an outlet for talent to shine.

At times, the projects chosen seemed surprising, and I wondered how a heavy metal band or a jewelry designer aligned with IBB's mission to advance knowledge and empower progress across the Middle East and Afghanistan. But journalism teaches you that the story is the person, not the project, and the remarkable ways they achieve their goals. Meeting these innovators, I have encountered sensitive solutions to local challenges, bringing hope and prosperity where they are needed most. Their enthusiasm is infectious, and I share their faith in a better future as they replace barriers with opportunity and realize long-held dreams of progress.

Olivia Cuthbert
Journalist and senior writer
at Ideas Beyond Borders

IDEAS BEYOND BORDERS

People of the Innovation Hub

Ideas Beyond Borders would not exist but for its people. We thank everyone and every partner of ours for all they have done and continue to do for this mission.

Program

Faisal Al Mutar - President and Co-founder of Ideas Beyond Borders

Rob Granieri - Program co-founder

Melissa Chen - Managing director

Rafal Al Adilee - MENA project manager

Ahmad Mansoor Ramizy - Program director, Afghanistan

Hussein Ibrahim - Head of Kurdistan office

Wameeth Al Shibi - Head of Iraq office

Issam Fawaz - Data and communications manager

Communications

Mariana Bernardez – Creative director

Reid Newton – Lead editor

Olivia Cuthbert – Senior writer

Advisors

Tyler Cowen

Rob Granieri

Printed in Great Britain
by Amazon